THE WILD, WILD WEST

For the Discriminating
 *Reader*

A chilling Illustrated History presenting

THE FACTS

about a PASSEL of low-down mischievous personages including

JOAQUÍN MURIETA, WILD BILL HICKOK,

JESSE JAMES, BAT MASTERSON,

WYATT EARP, & BILLY THE KID

Some were Lawmen, Some were Desperadoes, Some Began by **KILLING** and proceeded to **THEFT** and finally sank to telling **UNTRUTHS;**

Some TOYED with WEAK WOMEN like

CALAMITY JANE & BELLE STARR;

but all (HIDEOUS TO RELATE) gambled, swore, drank hard spirits, bragged, consorted with infamous **CHARACTERS**

and brought their Reputations to

✳ SHAME ✳

Herein An Honest Accounting of these so-called

HEROES OF THE FRONTIER

Together with a Stern Indictment of Those who have

exploited their evil-doing for

PROFIT & PELF

Painstakingly assembled by

PETER LYON

& now

FEARLESSLY published, Complete in One Volume,

by Funk and Wagnalls, of New York City

PICTURE CREDITS: *The Bettmann Archive,* pp. 22, 37, 90, 99, 105, 110, 116, 120, 122, 133; *Culver Pictures,* pp. 42, 44, 60, 80, 88, 94, 102, 136; *Collection of Margot Gayle,* pp. 50, 54; *The Granger Collection,* pp. 23, 30, 32, 78; *The New York Public Library,* pp. 14, 15, 27, 29, 39, 56, 64, 68, 70, 72, 74, 85, 86, 112, 125, 126, 129, 138, 139, 140, 142, 144.

*To the brave explorers and scouts who crossed the rivers
and scaled the mountains and searched the wilderness,
To the God-fearing farmers
who broke the plains with their plows
and civilized them with their sweat and their faith,*

*To the immigrants from the old world who settled west of
the Mississippi and,
using their fire-arms only to kill game,
contemptuously ignored the
nativist American "ethic" of violence,
This book is gratefully inscribed*

CONTENTS

LIST OF ILLUSTRATIONS

We crossed the sand-hills near the scene of the Indian mail robbery and massacre of 1856, wherein the driver and conductor perished, and also all the passengers but one, it was supposed; but this must have been a mistake, for at different times afterward on the Pacific coast I was personally acquainted with a hundred and thirty-three or four people who were wounded during that massacre, and barely escaped with their lives. There was no doubt of the truth of it—I had it from their own lips. One of these parties told me that he kept coming across arrow-heads in his system for nearly seven years after the massacre; and another of them told me that he was stuck so literally full of arrows that after the Indians were gone and he could raise up and examine himself, he could not restrain his tears, for his clothes were completely ruined.

Mark Twain, ROUGHING IT

The unrestfulness, the passion for speculation, the feverish eagerness for quick and showy results, may so soak into the texture of the popular mind as to colour it for centuries to come. There are the shadows which to the eye of the traveller seem to fall across the glowing landscape of the Great West.

James Bryce, THE AMERICAN COMMONWEALTH

AN INTRODUCTORY NOTE

When this exploration into one aspect of our national folklore was first undertaken it was informed with a two-fold purpose. One was to examine the legendary heroes of the Wild, Wild West and, on the basis of the historical evidence, to try to establish how accurate was the image presented of these heroes in the movies, on television, and in magazines and books. The other was to suggest how these popular media, and especially television, pandered to the wickedest impulses in their vast audiences by singling out and emphasizing the bloody violence which, it was maintained, was at the heart and gizzard of the legend.

13

If it could be demonstrated that the legend was false as well as evil, then, it was to be hoped, perhaps the men who make decisions about the content of the popular media might just conceivably cease and desist from intruding the slaughter house into the living room. Television was, for obvious reasons, by all odds the worst offender.

As I recall it, the impetus behind this effort was supplied by the editors of *American Heritage,* in whose pages the results of the exploration first appeared (in a much shorter and rather different form), and who are of course professionally interested in seeking to free the stream of American history of all garbage, raw sewage, and other pollutants. I am happy to accord them the deserved credit for their conception of the idea.

A Navy Colt

The *American Heritage* article itself stirred up a gratifying buzz of comment in newspapers (and on radio and television news programs) across the country, and likewise brought me considerably more mail than I was accustomed to.

The first shower of letters came from the gun buffs, all of whom appeared to be fanatically knowledgeable in the arcana of antique weaponry. (One of them subscribed himself as an "M/L buff," a phrase which I finally deciphered as meaning an expert in muzzle-loading firearms.) I had been so ill-advised as to write of a time that was "clouded by the black gunsmoke of all those Navy Colt .45s," and my correspondents were all eager to inform me (1) that there was and is no such thing as a Navy Colt .45, and (2) that the black powder of the day, when it was ignited, showed white smoke, not black. Here was an indisputable blunder, the inevitable howler that he who sets out confidently to correct error is bound to make. So far as I am aware, however, this was the only mistake in the work as originally printed. (I hasten to add that there are probably others, equally egregious, of which I have yet to be informed.)

A smaller shower of letters came next from writers, mostly of Wild West entertainments and mostly resident in southern California, all of whom were choleric to the point of apoplexy. To downgrade the Wild West was apparently to flick these artists on a raw nerve. From first to last my article, they insisted, was shamefully false. I had probably undertaken it, they hinted, for sordid pecuniary gain. "Inordinate lust for a dollar is a sorry thing," one of them wrote. (The editor of *American Heritage*, who knew what I had been paid, was happily able to nail this foul suggestion.) *"An outright lie,"* shrilled a Hollywood writer, of a statement he had misread. I had "deliberately falsified" my material or else I was "guilty of impossibly inadequate research." This same fellow, an author of Western novels, filled nearly thirty column-inches of the *Los Angeles Times*'s literary section with an intemperate onslaught on my essay, the whole being based on an oafish misreading of what I had written. He had apparently been so outraged by my demonstration of the patent absurdity of the Wild West legends that he could not properly read the words I

A Colt .45

had written. Further, he attributed to me material which I had quoted from another writer as an example of outlandish and reprehensible fantasy, and proceeded to savage me for having written it.

All this was sufficiently amusing and, if at any time I found myself in danger of taking it seriously, I could remind myself of the note that had come from J. Frank Dobie, the much-loved and well-respected Texas historian. He wrote: "I didn't feel that my mind was being insulted in reading this . . . excellent article." Professor Dobie also wrote: "You will not affect the public. The public wants to be fooled . . . concerning blackguards set up as heroes." While this was wise and true, it also served to put in question of how much use the article would be in ridding the air of programs that were worthless historically and vicious as public entertainments. Has anything happened to television programming, in the years since the article first appeared? Superficially, not much; fundamentally, nothing at all. Gone are most of the Western shows, so-called, that fraudulently pretended to be based on historical fact—the shows featuring actors spuriously made up to represent Bat Masterson, Wyatt Earp, Wild Bill

15

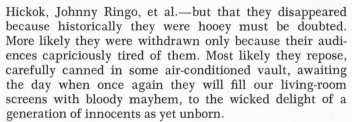

Hickok, Johnny Ringo, et al.—but that they disappeared because historically they were hooey must be doubted. More likely they were withdrawn only because their audiences capriciously tired of them. Most likely they repose, carefully canned in some air-conditioned vault, awaiting the day when once again they will fill our living-room screens with bloody mayhem, to the wicked delight of a generation of innocents as yet unborn.

Meanwhile, an organization called the National Association for Better Broadcasting has hung out its shingle in Los Angeles, the world's capital of commercial television, and has presumed to monitor the electronic output of three networks and x independent stations on a regular basis, testing whether or no this output is fit to look upon. (One might think that the job should more properly be done by the Federal Communications Commission, a government body supposedly responsive to the citizens of the Republic. But in the nature of things the F.C.C. answers only to Congress and to the networks of broadcasters, i.e., to the broadcasters.)

In the revulsion of horror and shame that followed the murder first of Martin Luther King, Jr., and then of Robert F. Kennedy, the N.A.B.B. made a list of the ten television programs "most detrimental" for youngsters; for a wonder, only three of the ten were Westerns. In the same period of national grief, officials of the three networks announced that their schedules were being closely examined, and that all producers had been instructed to bid their writers to scrub the violence from all programs then in production. A nationally syndicated columnist proudly proclaimed that, "in response to our columns on TV violence," the nasty stuff was being de-escalated, step-by-step, and would soon disappear forever from the nation's living rooms.

This flurry of hopeful activity turned out, however, to be only a brief pang of conscience. Two months later the N.A.B.B., having monitored the network and local stations in Los Angeles, reported that one hundred and ninety-five hours of "crime and horror programs, war films, and violent cartoons" were broadcast within a single week.

Finally, it should be noted that a Western program which was introduced on television after this author's article was originally published has, through sheer merit, been able to win a place on the N.A.B.B.'s list of the ten worst, the ten "most detrimental" on the score of violence. Its name: The Wild, Wild West.

PETER LYON

Woodstock, N.Y
April, 1969

17

THE WILD, WILD WEST

CHAPTER 1

THE WORLD OF THE

WILD, WILD WEST

The world of the Wild, Wild West is an odd world, internally consistent in its own cockeyed way, complete with a history, an ethic, a language, wars, a geography, a code, and a costume. The history is compounded of lies, the ethic was based on evil, the language was composed largely of argot and cant, the wars were fought by gangs of greedy gunmen, the geography was elastic, and the code and costume were both designed to accommodate violence. Yet this sinful world is, by any test, the most popular ever to be described to an American audience. Thousands of books have been written about it, many of them purporting to be history or biography; all but a very few are fiction,

Both code and costume were designed...

and rubbish to boot. It has, of course, afforded wondrously rich pickings for the journeymen of the mass entertainments; scores of writers for pulp magazines, motion pictures, comic strips, radio, and television have hacked their way over its trails. Even artists of the first rank have drawn upon it—Mark Twain reported as fact some grisly rumors about one of its heroes, Aaron Copland composed the music for a ballet that glorified its most pathological killer, Puccini wrote an opera about it, George Bernard Shaw confected an exceedingly silly play about it.

Nor has the world of the Wild, Wild West yet disappeared. It is still around, over thataway just a piece, bounded on three sides by credulity and on the fourth by the television screen. It will never disappear. The one power that might have tamed the Wild, Wild West is

... to accommodate violence

Truth, but over the last century Truth has shown herself to be laughably ineffectual. She is, indeed, long since dead, shot down by the blazing six-guns of Wild Bill Hickok, Wyatt Earp, Bat Masterson, Billy the Kid, and a dozen others, and her corpse lies mouldering somewhere on the Great Plains, in an unmarked grave.

Any discussion of the conquest of the West may be likened to an animated gabble down the length of a long dinner table, with several persons talking at once. At the head of the table, above the salt, where the historians have gathered, the talk is studied and thoughtful and focuses on events of weighty consequence. One man mentions the discovery of precious metals, which inspired adventurers by the scores of thousands to flock first to California, and later to Nevada, Colorado, Montana, Dakota, and Arizona. Another man tells of the Homestead Act of May, 1862, under the terms of which, within a generation, three hundred and fifty thousand hardy souls each carved a one-hundred-and-sixty-acre farm out of raw prairie. A third speaks of the railroads that were a-building, four of them linking, by 1884, the Mississippi Valley to the Pacific Coast. When it comes to the Indians, the historians all wag their heads dolefully, for while the oldest among them may once have referred glibly to the pacification of the savage aborigines, they are by now all agreed that the westward expansion came about only by virtue of Indian treaties cynically violated and Indian territory shamelessly seized. The picture that emerges from their talk is one of gruelling hard work; of explorers and trappers and bearded prospectors; of Chinese coolies toiling east and Irish immigrants toiling west, laying track across wilderness; of farmers with hands as hard as horn, sheltered from the blizzards and the northers only by sod huts; of ranchers and longhorn cattle and cowboys weary in the saddle. The quality evoked by their talk is of enduring courage, the greater because it is largely anonymous. The smell that hangs over their talk is of sweat.

But at the foot of the table, below the salt, where sit the chroniclers of the Wild, Wild West, the talk is shrill and excited, and the smell that hangs overhead is of gunpowder. For here the concern is with men of dash and derring-do, and the picture that emerges from the talk is of gaudy cowtowns and slambang mining camps: curious settlements, in which the only structures are saloons, gambling halls, dance palaces, whorehouses, burlesque theaters, and jails; in which there are no people, but only heroes and villains, all made of papier-mâché, all wearing six-guns, and all (except for the banker) with hearts of 22-karat gold. In this never-never land, the super-hero is the gunslinger, the man who can draw fastest and shoot straightest; in brief, the killer. Sometimes he swaggers along the wooden sidewalks with a silver star pinned to his shirt—a sheriff or a United States marshal. Before he wore the star he may have been a professional gambler, road agent, buffalo hunter, bank robber, cattle rustler, Indian scout, horse thief, stagecoach driver, or murderer, or he may have been, trivially enough, simply the town bully. He may be any of these again (sometimes without troubling to unpin his badge). But when he wore the star—so runs the argument—he tamed the Wild, Wild West, he brought and enforced law and order.

As we shall presently see, no argument could lead further from the truth. For the moment it will be enough to note that, whether he was outlaw or officer of the law, if he applied himself diligently to the smashing of the Ten Commandments, with special attention to the Sixth—that is, if he was a sufficiently ugly, evil, and murderous killer—he was in a way to become a storied American hero.

We propose to trundle a half-dozen of these paragons up for inspection at close range. This sextet—three outlaws and three peace officers: Joaquín Murieta, Billy the Kid, and Jesse James; Wild Bill Hickok, Bat Masterson, and Wyatt Earp—has been carefully culled on the basis not only of proven popularity over the years but also of present *réclame*. Nor will the ladies be ignored: we will ask Calamity Jane, and Belle Starr, the Bandit Queen, to curtsey briefly. And we will spend a brief while in Abilene, a cowtown of some repute.

If we are obliged to ignore such notables as Sheet Iron Jack, Kettle-Belly Johnson, the Verdigris Kid, Fly-Specked Billy, Hoodoo Brown, and Madame Moustache, it is only because, alas! they never engaged a sufficiently enterprising press agent. Regrettable; as is the twilight of Persimmon Bill, Hurricane Bill, Whiskey Bill, Curly Bill, Flopping

The sod hut was a common form of luxury

Bill, and Ranicky Bill. Good gunmen all, but with no sense of posterity.

But before entering our gallery of papier-mâché horribles, it may be instructive to reflect upon the technique by which an uproariously bad man can acquire a reputation that is at once inflated, grisly, and prettified. This will require some small knowledge of the economics of the Wild, Wild West and a brief peek at the sources available to the chroniclers of this hazy world, this world so clouded by the gunsmoke of all those Colt .45s.

There were, broadly speaking, two ways of making money in the West. One, as has been suggested, demanded hard, hard work, that of farmer, cowhand, railroader, or miner. But as always seems to be the case in this bad old world, there were some few men who did not care for hard work. Either they had tried it personally, for a day or two, and found it repugnant, or they had conceived a distaste for it by watching others try it, or perhaps they had simply heard about others who had tried it and so come to a bad end. In any case, these men determined never to work but to rely, rather, on their wits.

Now how could a quick-witted man make a bundle, out on the bare, bleak plains? Clearly the first step was to head for those outposts of civilization, however malodorous to a discriminating rogue, where a little heap of wealth had been piled up through the labor of others. This meant the cowtowns, the mining camps, and the slowly shifting railroad settlements. Here he could gamble with the chumps: few professional gamblers starve. Here he could pimp: whores were in even greater demand west of the Mississippi than east of it. Here he could, if he were well enough connected or if he had a small dab of capital to venture, buy a share of a dancehall or saloon: either enterprise was gilt-edged. Before long he would have found, as others have before and since, that these careers led straight into politics. He might have concluded that it was cheaper to stand for office himself than to fork over a monotonous handful of cash, week after week, to some stupider, lazier politician. So were marshals and sheriffs born.

But what of the dull-witted man who didn't choose to

work? He had behind him, typically, a life of violence bred by the Civil War; often his thick skull held no learning whatever save how to ride, shoot, kill, burn, rob, rape, and run. With the end of the war he doffed his blue blouse or, more often, his gray, and headed west toward a short, gory life of bank heists and train robberies. So were outlaws born.

Rounding up cattle for the trail

The quick-witted man could live off the chumps

For the man who was preternaturally active and had no
objection to a day in the outdoors, there was a third,
coarsening, semi-legal path to quick dollars: he could
slaughter bison. Only the Indians would object, and who
cared a hoot for the Indians? A treaty of 1867 guaranteed
that no white man would hunt buffalo south of the Arkansas River; by 1870, when the army officer commanding
Fort Dodge was asked what he would do if this promise

Splendid practice
for killers

were broken, he laughed and said: "Boys, if I were hunting buffalo I would go where buffalo are." By 1871, since buffalo hides were worth $2.25 apiece, the massacre began in earnest. One hunter bagged 5,855 in two months. It has been estimated that 4,373,730 bison were killed in the three years 1872 to 1874. To shoot the placid beasts was no easier than shooting fish in a barrel, but it was certainly no more difficult. And splendid practice: as safe as on a target range, for the marksman who might later choose to pot riskier game, such as a stagecoach driver or the leader of a posse. So were killers trained.

It remained only to make over all these sheriffs, outlaws, and killers into heroes. Considering the material on hand to work with, this transfiguration is on the order of a major miracle. It was brought about in two ways.

Firstly, whilst the assorted pluguglies were still alive, hosannas were raised in their honor (1) by *The National Police Gazette,* a lively weekly edited from 1877 to 1922 by Richard K. Fox and commanding a circulation that reached into every self-respecting barber shop, billiard parlor, barroom, and bagnio throughout the republic, and (2) by each impressionable journalist, from the more genteel Eastern newspapers and magazines, who had wangled enough expense money out of his publisher to waft him west of Wichita. Fox required no authentication and desired none; his staff writers simply pitched their stuff out by the forkful, to be engorged by yokels wherever, from Fifth Avenue to Horner's Corners. The aforesaid round-eyed journalists, on the other hand, got their stuff straight from the gunfighters themselves (or from the gunfighters' loved ones), so naturally it was deemed wholly reliable.

Secondly, about a generation ago, after the assorted pluguglies had been gathered to their everlasting sleep, the latter-day chroniclers crept eagerly in. They (or at least a few of them) would be careful and scholarly; they would write nothing, so they swore, that was not verified either by an oldtimer who knew whereof he spoke from personal knowledge or by a contemporary newspaper account. Thus, whatever they printed would be the truth, the whole truth, etcetera.

One flaw in this admirable approach was that the contemporary newspaper accounts were not reliable. How could they be, when the newspapers themselves were flaring examples of the sort of personal journalism in which personal bias as to local politics and local personalities customarily displaced respect for facts? The feuds that erupted into the celebrated "wars" of the Wild, Wild West —such affrays as the Lincoln County War, the Johnson County War, or the shooting in the O.K. Corral—were essentially struggles to seize political and economic power in an anarchic arena. They were contested as crudely as the street urchins' game of King-of-the-Mountain, in which the sole law is the hard fist. In such a struggle no local newspaper could stand uncommitted and exist. Moreover, any halfway independent and intelligent reporter for the newspapers of the Wild West fully appreciated that, when he wrote about the gunmen of his community, he was describing an interconnected underworld, a brotherhood that embraced outlaw, politician, and sheriff quite as amicably— and cautiously—as does the latter-day brotherhood of gangster and corrupt police official in the big cities of our own time. Such an insight naturally flavored the contemporary newspaper accounts of the feats of heroes like Wyatt Earp or Mysterious Dave Mather.

The other flaw was that the stories of oldtimers come not from personal knowledge of what happened so much as from the files of the imaginative *National Police Gazette*. Venerable nesters could be found all over the Southwest, fifty years after the timely deaths of Billy the Kid or Jesse James or Belle Starr, clamoring to testify to the boyish charm of the one, the selfless nobility of the other, and the amorous exploits of the third. Their memories were all faithful transcripts of the *Gazette*'s nonsense. Its editor's classic formula for manufacturing heroes had so effectively retted the minds of his readers that they could never thereafter disentangle fiction from fact.

Analysis of this Fox formula for heroes reveals that it has ten ingredients, like a Chinese soup:

1. The hero's accuracy with any weapon is prodigious.
2. He is a nonpareil of bravery and courage.
3. He is courteous to all women, regardless of rank, station, age, or physical charm.
4. He is gentle, modest, and unassuming.
5. He is handsome, sometimes even pretty, so that he seems even feminine in appearance; but withal he is of course very masculine, and exceedingly attractive to women.
6. He is blue-eyed. His piercing blue eyes turn gray as steel (or flint) when he is aroused; his associates would have been well advised to keep a color chart handy, so that

they might have dived for a storm-cellar when the blue turned to tattle-tale gray.

7. He was driven to a life of outlawry and crime by having quite properly defended a loved one from an intolerable affront—with lethal consequences. Thereafter, however,

8. He shields the widow and orphan, robbing only the banker or railroad monopolist.

9. His death comes about by means of betrayal or treachery, but

10. It is rarely a conclusive death, since he keeps bobbing up later on, in other places, for many years. It is, indeed, arguable whether he is dead yet.

With these attributes in mind, let us roll forward the first exhibit, which is as blurred as an eighth carbon copy, since, for reasons that will presently become clear, no authentic picture of this bandit exists. It is labeled

 MURIETA

CHAPTER 2

JOAQUÍN MURIETA

After gold was discovered in California, there were, no doubt about it, brigands from one end of the Mother Lode to the other. Since Mexicans—having got to the goldfields first—were exceedingly unpopular with the Americans, English, and Australians who greedily hustled to the region, naturally it was put about that the dastardly malefactors were exclusively Mexican. Joaquín being a common Mexican name, it followed that many of the desperadoes must be called Joaquín. And so it turned out.

Joseph Henry Jackson, the California historian with a most beguiling affection for the truth, turned up five Joaquíns in various dusty files, with various patronyms,

thus: Murieta, Carillo, Valenzuela, Ocomorenia, and Botel-
lier (or Botilleras)—each an allegedly bona fide bandit.
Did any of them actually exist? At this distance, it is hard
to say. At any rate, in the early 1850s, it was Murieta who
collared most of the glory for the gory exploits that made a
Californian's each particular hair to stand an end, like quills
upon the fretful porpentine. If a Chinese throat were slit in
Placerville, it must be Murieta! And if on the same night a
stagecoach were robbed two hundred miles away in Visalia,
no matter—it was Murieta!

Now what can be discerned here is, of course, that
familiar monster with blood of black ink and bones of
headline type which is confected by playful reporters
whenever hard news is scarce. But it is a monster that can
terrify, nonetheless—Murieta was journalistically endowed with a bloodthirsty lieutenant called Manuel (Three-
Fingered Jack) García. As the list of his reported crimes
mounted, a hue and cry went up which, by May, 1853,
sensibly affected the politicians in the Assembly of the
infant state. A resolution was passed authorizing a trans-
planted Texan, one Harry Love, to form a company of
rangers, at a monthly wage of one hundred and fifty
dollars apiece, and lead them into the hills to capture
Joaquín. Which Joaquín was not specified; any Joaquín
would serve if only the hullabaloo about Joaquín would die
down. The politicians belatedly asserted some common
sense: Love's rangers would be paid for only three months.
Governor Bigler himself put up an additional one thousand
dollars for Joaquín, dead or alive. The Mexican, if he
existed, had not been tried, examined, or convicted of anything; but he was now to be hunted down by a posse of
men well-paid for their work.

Love acted in quite predictable fashion. That is, he rode
to and fro through the hills for nearly three months and
then picked a fight with some Mexicans. (At any rate, his
rangers did; there is some doubt as to whether Love was on
hand for the fight.) On July 30, 1853, the San Francisco
Herald reported that "the famous bandit, Joaquín, whose
name is associated with a hundred deeds of blood, has at
last been captured" after a desperate fight in the wilds of
Tulare Valley at a place called Panoche Pass. In proof of
his capture—and to claim the one-thousand-dollar bounty

Malefactors in California were exclusively Mexican

—Love proffered the head of a Mexican, pickled in a jug of spirits, and, as a kind of lagniappe, a three-fingered hand, allegedly that of Manuel, also pickled. These gruesome objects were promptly exhibited by various showmen in saloons throughout the region. The legislature, moved no doubt solely by a profound sense of gratitude, presently voted Love an additional five thousand dollars. The doughty captain nevertheless soon after died, a paranoiac, shooting it out with a posse he imagined to be his lifelong enemies.

Meantime the editor of the San Francisco *Alta California* deemed it time to blow the whistle on all this nonsense. "Joaquín," he wrote, "is a fabulous character only, and this is widely known." Too late. Someone invented a story about an alleged sister of Murieta's, who came to inspect the jugged head and thereafter denied that it was her Joaquín. Murieta may never have lived in fact, but he was by now vigorously alive in legend, and he would never die.

Joseph Henry Jackson has traced the provenance of the legend to a potboiling thriller written in 1854 by a half-Cherokee journalist named John Rollin (Yellow Bird) Ridge. Joaquín, Ridge wrote, had been driven to a life of crime when a gang of American miners ravished his bride, Rosita, hanged his brother, and beat Joaquín himself until, as a subsequent mythmaker put it, "He lay insensible, from head to foot one mass of blood." The California *Police Gazette* added to the legend, so did the Beadle Dime Library. An awful poet named Cincinnatus Heine Miller wrote a long and awful poem called "Joaquín" and it so delighted him that he changed his name to Joaquín Miller. He asserted that Rosita was a direct descendant of Montezuma. Someone else, citing "new historical evidence," claimed that Murieta had been Santa Anna's bodyguard. Joaquín was, it was said, never without his copies of Cervantes and Racine; he was brave, courteous, gentle, handsome; he had never died, but gone home to Sonora, in Mexico; no, to Chile; no, to Castile. His love's name was not Rosita, it was Carmela; no, it was Clarina. In 1932 there appeared a biography that laced all these lies into one superb whopper: it was called *The Robin Hood of El*

Dorado; the Saga of Joaquín Murrieta [sic]. It was such a charlotte russe that it was of course at once snapped up by Hollywood, whence it presently issued as a film, heaving under still another blanket of whipped cream, and starring Warner Baxter.

Murieta is now so firmly fixed in all the histories that have been written about California that he can never be dislodged. Perhaps he belongs there.

But we cannot leave the West Coast without paying our respects to an authentic California bandit: Black Bart, who should be everybody's favorite road agent. From 1877 to 1883 Black Bart held up twenty-eight stage coaches, and his technique never varied. He would appear alone, by a lonely stretch of road, carrying a rifle, wearing a long white duster, and with his head encased in a flour sack in which eyeholes had been cut. In a voice described as "deep and hollow" he would order the driver: "Throw down the box!" Then he would bid the driver to be off, and would loot the box at his leisure. He never had to use his gun.

After Black Bart's fourth robbery, the Wells Fargo people found that he had left a scrap of paper in the box. On the paper was written:

> I've labored long and hard for bread,
> For honor and for riches,
> But on my corns too long you've tred,
> You fine-haired sons of bitches.

This was signed "Black Bart, the Po 8." Po 8? What cabalistic symbol was this? Before long the sleuths deduced that Black Bart was suggesting that he was the author of Po 8ry and, sure enough, a few robberies later he left another scrap of paper:

> Here I lay me down to sleep
> To wait the coming morrow
> Perhaps success, perhaps defeat
> And everlasting sorrow . . .
> Let come what will I'll try it on
> My condition can't be worse
> And if there's money in that box
> 'Tis munny in my purse.

Black Bart sans white duster and flour sack

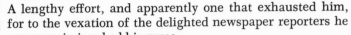

A lengthy effort, and apparently one that exhausted him, for to the vexation of the delighted newspaper reporters he never again invoked his muse.

By mischance, his twenty-eighth holdup led to his downfall and he was arrested in San Francisco, where he was living as Charles E. Bolton, an apparently respectable and prosperous mining engineer. On the flyleaf of the Bible in his apartment, a detective noticed the name Charles E. Boles. When he was arraigned, Black Bart stoutly gave his name as T. Z. Spaulding. He was asked what was his education. "Liberal!" he snapped. He was sent to San Quentin. He behaved himself and was, after a few years, released on parole. When he strolled out, he was at once surrounded by reporters. The interview proceeded along well-worn lines. Was it back to a life of crime? Certainly not. What did he plan to do? None of your business. Presently Boles turned away; but one reporter, persistent, asked: "Maybe you'll be writing some more poetry?" Boles swung around. "Young man," he said sternly, "didn't you hear me say I'd given up a life of crime?"

But it is time to turn to our second major exhibit—a man narrow-waisted and wide-hipped, with small hands and feet, whose curly golden hair tumbles to his shoulders—in sum, a man who looks like a male impersonator. His label reads

 HICKOK

Wild Bill—admired by tagtails and tufthunters

CHAPTER 3

James (Wild Bill) Butler Hickok was born on a farm in La Salle County, Illinois, on May 27, 1837, the fourth of six children. He died on the afternoon of August 2, 1876, in Saloon Number Ten, on the main street of Deadwood, in the Dakota Territory, when a bullet fired by Jack McCall ploughed through the back of his head, coming out through his cheek and smashing a bone in the left forearm of a Captain Massey, a riverboat pilot with whom Hickok had been playing poker. During his lifetime, Hickok did some remarkable deeds, and they were even more remarkably embroidered by himself and by a corps of admiring tagtails and tufthunters. When he died, he held two pair—aces and eights—a legendary combination known ever since as "the dead man's hand." It is the least of the legends that has encrusted his reputation, like barnacles on an old hulk.

Was he brave? His most critical biographer, William E. Connelley, has said that fear "was simply a quality he lacked."

Was he handsome? He was "the handsomest man west of the Mississippi. His eyes were blue—but could freeze to a cruel steel-gray at threat of evil or danger."

Was he gallant? His morals were "much the same as those of Achilles, King David, Lancelot, and Chevalier Bayard, though his amours were hardly as frequent as David's or as inexcusable as Lancelot's."

Had he no minor vices? Very few: "Wild Bill found relaxation and enjoyment in cards but he seldom drank."

Could he shoot? Once in Solomon, Kansas, a pair of murderers fled from him. "One was running up the street and the other down the street in the opposite direction. Bill fired at both men simultaneously and killed them both." Presumably with his eyes closed. Again, in Topeka, in 1870, Buffalo Bill Cody threw his hat into the air as a target. "Wild Bill shot an evenly spaced row of holes along the outside of the rim as it was falling, and before it touched the ground."*

But surely he was modest? Yes, indeed. "Faced with admirers, he blushed and stammered and fled."

Was he a sure-enough killer? Once he was asked how many white men he had killed, to his certain knowledge. (Indians didn't count.) Wild Bill reflected. "I suppose," he said at last, "I have killed considerably over a hundred." But this was in 1866; he would have another ten years to improve his record. To another reporter, he remarked: "As to killing men, I never think much about it. . . . The killing of a bad man shouldn't trouble one any more than killing a rat or an ugly cat or a vicious dog." Of course, it helps if one is as good a judge as Hickok was of the badness of a man, or the ugliness of a cat.

* To fully appreciate this miracle of marksmanship, one must remember that Hickok was shooting black-powder cartridges. (Smokeless powder did not come into general use until about 1893.) Each time he fired, therefore, he put a puff of white smoke between himself and his target. After his first shot, he could have seen his target only with difficulty. But then, nothing is impossible to the gunslinger of the Wild West.

But was a good man not obliged to kill bad men, to tame the Wild West? And, after all, was Wild Bill not a pillar of righteousness in those sinful times? What about his lustrous reputation as marshal of the Kansas cowtowns? Hickok was, perhaps, a United States deputy marshal operating out of Fort Riley in February, 1866, charged with rounding up deserters and horse thieves; but the record of his tenure is fuzzy.

In mid-August, 1869, he was elected sheriff of Ellis County—of which Hays was the biggest town—to fill an unexpired term. In November, he failed to be re-elected. A brief time in which to tame a tough town, nor does the record show any notable success. He may have killed a man named Jack (or Sam) Strawhorn (or Strawhan) who tried to get the drop on him; he may have killed two soldiers who talked tough at him; he may have thrashed Tom Custer, a brother of General George Custer; he may have killed three soldiers whom Custer had vengefully sic'ed on him—all the evidence bearing on these matters is likewise fuzzy. What is certain is that Hickok left Hays in a hurry, one winter night, lest he be further beset by the Seventh Cavalry.

In April, 1871, Hickok was appointed marshal of Abilene, and now the picture grows sharper. It was an auspicious conjunction of man and town: each was at the height of notoriety.

As for the town, which was, in a formal sense, not yet two years old, 1871 would be its peak year as a cowtown: six hundred thousand cattle would pass through its yards on the way to Eastern markets; and all that summer cowboys by the hundreds would jam its dancehalls and saloons —the Alamo, the Bull's Head, the Elkhorn, the Pearl, the Old Fruit, the Trail, and the Red Front—to squander a year's wages.

As for the man . . . but perhaps, before returning to the man, it would be as well to sketch the town in greater detail, for a more precise history and description of Abilene will serve as an illuminating backdrop for all the other Kansas cowtowns—Ellsworth, Wichita, Caldwell, Newton, Dodge City—and so, in tonic fashion, work to dispel some part of the phony romance, the sentimentality, and the cumbersome myths that have, in sticky combination, obscured a remarkable aspect of American economic history. Such an approach will necessitate an inquiry into when and where, and how and why, the cowtown was born. But no student should despair: the course of study will include villainy and farce and sin, and it will yet be inspired by the virtues of industry, imagination, and religious faith. In short, it will be a thoroughly American tale.

Where Abilene would be, there was, at first, only a gentle roll of upland prairie and the broad, shallow bottomland of a small, muddy, plains river, later to be called the Smoky Hill. This stream, bordered by cottonwoods and fed by desultory creeks, swung in long lazy curves which showed that the river had still to cut a deep and lasting channel. The first settler in the vicinity cleared some farmland alongside what he aptly called Mud Creek, and here in the summer of 1857 he built a log cabin. A couple of years later, with government assistance, this man had built a stone stable and was operating a station for the Butterfield Overland Dispatch. By 1861 a land speculator had bought a tract of real estate, had divided it into visionary blocks and lots, and, taking his cue from one inspired by Holy Writ (Luke III, 1), had dubbed it Abilene. Not long afterward this dreamer, in a newspaper advertisement emblazoned "HO! HO! FOR THE WEST," alleged that his town already boasted "a store, blacksmith shop, hotel, Post Office, and several families."

For the next five years nothing much happened in Abilene, except that a westbound railroad track was laid alongside, and swiftly past, the settlement. Abilene was not deemed of sufficient status to be a train-stop. Its depot was a plank on a sawhorse; mail was gathered in or flung off without pause. The railroad's promoters, their greedy eyes glistening at the chance to grab huge land-grants if only they could lay track as far as Colorado by 1870, had pressed on posthaste toward Salina.

In the spring of 1867, eagerly traveling over this railroad on a pass, came a tall, lanky, gawky, young man called Joseph McCoy. The youngest of three brothers, he was impatient, sanguine, pertinacious, his mind expanding with a dream that kept him hustling by day and wakeful at night. The train was unexpectedly obliged to stop at Abilene for an hour, while a bridge over one of the muddy streams was repaired. McCoy, itching with impatience, got off to look around. What he saw, he reported later, was "a very small, dead place, consisting of about one dozen log huts—low, small, rude affairs, four-fifths of which were covered with dirt for roofing." In short, Dullsville, in spades. And yet, the more that young McCoy learned about this wretched spot, the higher his spirits rose and the better, for his ambitious purposes, he considered it.

McCoy and his two older brothers were dealers in livestock—cattle, sheep, hogs, even mules—and McCoy was obsessed by the notion that there was a fortune to be made in the cattle business, if only he could work out the logistics of the thing. The law of supply-and-demand was most inviting: in the vast reaches of Texas there were known to be several million head of longhorn cattle which had been breeding and multiplying throughout the years of the Civil War, but up north and back east the citizenry were yearning for good beef. Down there a glut, and so a low selling price; up here a hunger, and so a high purchase price. What more propitious moment to step in and make a market?

And yet there was no great rush of entrepreneurs into Kansas to profit from the cattle trade, and this because grave difficulties attended on the arrival of the Texas longhorn into any northern state. One: no sensible farmer wanted huge herds of cattle trampling his fields, eating his grass, and draining dry his watercourses. Two: bands of so-called bushwhackers (by which was meant gangs of lawless men, recently demobilized from the Confederate armies) preyed upon every cattle drover and every drove of cattle heading north from Texas. These gangs devoted themselves to highjacking the cattle and abusing, when they did not summarily kill, the drovers. Three, and most important: Texas longhorn cattle were believed to infect all shorthorn cattle with a mortal disease, variously called Texas fever, Spanish fever, or blackwater.

Where this fever came from or how it spread no man

Young Mr. McCoy, who reared up Abilene

knew, although there were theories aplenty.* One thing was certain: the fever fatally infected domestic cattle pastured with longhorns. When in 1866 there occurred an unusually severe epidemic, the legislators of Missouri, Kansas, Nebraska, Colorado, Kentucky, and Illinois all promptly passed laws forbidding or limiting the herding of Texas cattle across their state lines. "We should keep out the Texas cattle on the same principle that we would the small pox or the cholera," trumpeted the editor of one border-state newspaper. "They are pestilential." The complex Kansas statute seemed designed to restrict the longhorns to the southwestern quarter of the state, but it permitted certain interesting exceptions. McCoy later maintained that Abilene "was the farthest point east at which a good depot for cattle business could have been" established. Abilene was, in fact, well within the proscribed area, but, curiously, no one ever blew the whistle on McCoy's illegal cattle trade.

For the rest, Abilene was ideal for McCoy's purposes. The countryside roundabout was almost entirely unsettled; there was an abundance of streams; there was, for grazing, plenty of bluestem and buffalo grass; and land for stockyards could be cheaply bought. It remained only for McCoy to strike a deal with an officer of the railroad— with, no less, the president of the railroad, one John D. Perry.† Nothing could conceivably have been more seduc-

---

* The notion most diligently plugged by the veterinary scientists (and most derisively scorned by cattlemen) had to do with "a small egg, or sporule," supposedly deposited somehow on the blades of grass in Texas. Another school held that the fatal infection was in the longhorn's saliva or "slobbers," or in the urine, or in what was delicately described as the "residuum." Still other stockmen suspected cattle ticks, but they were unable to elucidate any chain of cause-and-effect. A generation later, entomologists of the Department of Agriculture (to whom all credit is due for the vigorous and profitable commerce in beef) would show that a parasitic protozoon was indeed transmitted by ticks into the bloodstream of cattle; to suppress the disease thereafter was relatively simple.

† The company was known, at this time, as the Union Pacific Railroad, Eastern Division; later it would be called the Kansas Pacific Railroad. Its reputation throughout its corporate history was less than lustrous. Having passed through the hands of some of the most fragrant scoundrels in American railroad history, the road was finally absorbed by the Union Pacific.

tive to Perry than the assurance of eastbound freight. He acknowledged as much to McCoy and proceeded to encourage him in the venture as follows: "We have no faith or confidence in your enterprise, and I tell you frankly and candidly that we regard it as the wildest, most chimerical, visionary, and impracticable project we ever heard of, and we will not put a dollar in it, nor be responsible for a dollar that anybody puts into it. . . . Preposterous! Ridiculous!" After which, Perry agreed to pay McCoy five dollars for each carload of cattle sent from Abilene to the Eastern markets.

On the strength of this promise (which Perry of course subsequently repudiated, and would honor only after two years of litigation) McCoy went back to Abilene and set in motion the changes that would, almost overnight, enable it to become one of the most celebrated small towns in the country. McCoy acted swiftly, shrewdly, imaginatively, and with an openhanded generosity. He was at once a promoter, a planner, a builder, and a fervent apostle. All his admirable qualities inevitably led to irreconcilable contradictions and landed him in financial disaster. The same would be the experience of other promoters in the other cowtowns of Kansas, from Abilene west to Dodge City; and each experience would afford the same paradigm of one of the oldest conflicts in the world, the one that set Cain against Abel.

Abel, it will be recalled, was "a keeper of sheep," whilst Cain was a farmer, "a tiller of the ground" (Genesis IV, 2). Biblical scholars, puzzling over the obscure violence in the dawn of man's history that led so suddenly to murder, have conjectured that the spare, lean verses of Genesis IV, 2–8 are a way of describing, in a mythic shorthand, the collision between two rivalrous economic systems: the nomadic and the agricultural. There was Abel, letting his herds wander to graze where they chose; and here was Cain, sweating to sow his seed and to harvest his fruit and his grain. Did Abel's sheep and cattle trample Cain's crops? And was that why "it came to pass, when they were in the field, that Cain rose up against Abel his brother, and slew him"? At all events, the same violent drama was often to be played out on the Western prairie.

McCoy began by buying several hundred acres of real estate in and around Abilene. (It came cheap, at less than eight dollars an acre.) Next—in remarkably short order, considering that he had to import both his building materials and the workmen who could put them together—he built the Great Western Stockyards, big enough to hold a thousand cattle; a barn; an office; a large livery stable; a bank; and a three-story frame hotel called the Drover's Cottage, which boasted plaster walls and such eye-popping splendors as venetian blinds, a billiards room, and ice for the drinks served in the bar. All these structures, and others like them, were put together in this part of the prairie, this drab and unprepossessing spot, this "very small, dead place," simply because north from Texas to Abilene led a trail. This trail would later be called the Chisholm Trail after the half-Scots, half-Indian trader, Jesse Chisholm, who first blazed that part of it that reached north from Texas through the Indian Territory (subsequently Oklahoma) and through Kansas up to the mouth of the Little Arkansas River.

McCoy had, of course, taken care to publicize his activities.—south, in Texas, among the wealthy cattlemen; east, in Missouri and Illinois, among the big butchers and meatpackers; and in person to the governor of Kansas, Samuel J. Crawford, who gave the enterprise his "semi-official" blessing despite its patent illegality. Governor Crawford took the broad commercial view and ignored the plaints of many apprehensive Kansas farmers. The governor refused to be daunted by the possibility that Texas fever might sicken someone else's domestic cattle. "I regard the opening of that cattle trail into and across western Kansas," he said, "of as much value to the state as is the Missouri River."

Even before McCoy's Great Western Stockyards were ready to receive them, herds of Texas cattle were waiting to be shipped; even before McCoy's hotel, the Drover's Cottage, was ready to feed them and bed them down, southern and northern cattlemen had gathered and were beginning to bargain. McCoy had created a market.

The officers of the Kansas Pacific, in the great tradition of American railroading, had grossly underestimated the

Part of the Drover's Cottage in Abilene. The rest was sawed off and shipped to Ellsworth, where a hotel was desperately needed

potential of Abilene and the cattle trade. Hastily they issued orders for the construction of a tiny depot, about the
size of a large packing-crate, and for the laying of tracks
for a siding big enough to shunt twenty stock cars.

(Within a year the siding would be big enough to accommodate one hundred stock cars, and the railroad officials, belatedly appreciating the facts of life, would be scrambling to stick slats on flat cars and so prepare to meet the

Cowboys
saddlng up

Frederic Remington

great rush of traffic.) In late August, 1867, McCoy held what he modestly described as "a monster cattle auction." Cattle were snapped up for the Eastern market at prices up to twenty-five dollars a head. The Texans were delighted.

McCoy, still a young man, still under thirty years of age, still capable of a boundless enthusiasm, laid on a banquet and celebration just as though he and his guests were not forlorn visitors to a dreary prairie. He put up a tent next to his unfinished hotel, he served fine foods, he poured the best wines available west of the Missouri. There were speeches. Later, McCoy wrote: "On the morning following the banquet, September 5, the iron horse was darting down the Kaw Valley with the first trainload of cattle that ever passed over the Kansas Pacific Railroad, the precursor to many thousands destined to follow." The first shipment filled twenty stock cars. McCoy was very confident of the future. Success lay ready at hand.

There was, however, one problem.

The Drover's Cottage stood and was about to be opened, swank, splendid, elegant, a sure symbol of success on the frontier, the most inviting hostelry on all the plains between the Missouri and the Rockies, and its custom was assured. The wealthy cattlemen would be taken care of. But what of the cowhands? What of the hungry young men, filthy from long nights on the trail, exhausted after fighting spring floods, Comanche raiders, occasional stampedes, and battles with outlaws? What of the lean young men looking for ease and relaxation, money in their pockets, lust in their loins, hoping for a half-share of happiness? They, too, would want accommodations: shops, restaurants, hotels, saloons; in short, they would want an instant city of the plain.

McCoy knew this. He knew it, and deep in his Presbyterian heart he hoped that his instant city of the plain would not suddenly become like unto a Sodom and a Gomorrah. Late in 1867 he spoke earnestly and persuasively to a young friend, an Illinois neighbor named Theodore Henry.

McCoy wanted Henry to help develop Abilene, to sell its real estate to solid, substantial merchants and settlers who would make the town into a thriving, respectable, God-fearing community and a center of agricultural commerce.

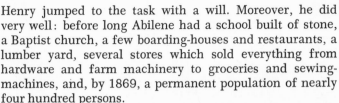

Henry jumped to the task with a will. Moreover, he did very well: before long Abilene had a school built of stone, a Baptist church, a few boarding-houses and restaurants, a lumber yard, several stores which sold everything from hardware and farm machinery to groceries and sewing-machines, and, by 1869, a permanent population of nearly four hundred persons.

What McCoy seems never to have realized is that, by his having summoned Baptist and other respectabilities, he had tolled the death knell over his cattle trade. It could not have been otherwise. A few hundred timid citizens were, for five months of the year, to be invested by a few hundred Texas cowboys exulting in their release from toil and danger, in their youthful spirits, and in the firepower of their six-guns. Add to them a transient population of another few score harpies—whores, saloon-keepers, gamblers, and their complicitous riff-raff—who descended on the town to relieve the cowboys of their sudden wages, and you have, for the timid, a very fair picture of Hell. Indeed, that is precisely how contemporary journalists saw it. In July, 1868, one of them noted in a Topeka newspaper: "At this writing, Hell is now in session in Abilene."

The summer of 1868 was, however, relatively staid. In 1868 only some seventy-five thousand head of cattle were trailed to Abilene; in 1869 that number was more than doubled, and matters in the town were at least twice as serious. They were, in fact, intolerable to all those who thought of themselves as decent people. A chief difficulty was that the decent and the indecent were all crowded together in one compact area: from the stockyards on the east to Mud Creek on the west was no more than a mile, and all the buildings in the town (save only for Joe McCoy's house) were, until 1870, built south of the railroad tracks. Virtuous women and sporting women shared the same plank sidewalks and perforce shopped at the same stores; the schoolhouse and the Baptist church were less than a block away from two of the gamier saloons, the Old Fruit and the Bull's Head. It was this last circumstance that most outraged the decent citizens and touched off a ludicrous controversy that provoked Abilene into reform and, ultimately, to the rejection of the cattle trade.

The owner of the Bull's Head, a Texan, commissioned a

Hurrahing a town

painter to depict, on a large sign affixed to the front of his
saloon, a big red bull, realistically represented, complete
with his pizzle. And why not? After all, bulls daily walked
the streets of Abilene, none of them being first required to
don pants. Nevertheless, the outcry was shrill and an-
guished. The sign was denounced as immoral: an insult to
good women, and a malign influence on innocent children
who were constrained to look at it on their way to school.
After two weeks of caterwauling, the sign was given a coat
of overpaint through which, however, the pizzle could still
be descried.

On the strength of this dubious victory, the forces for
reform marched forward. Why were the saloons not licensed? Why was prostitution not quelled forthwith or, at
the very least, likewise licensed? Why was there not law
and order in the town? Answer was made that, since the
town was not incorporated, law enforcement could be
provided only by county officials, who had found the task
impossible. Well, then, cried the reformers, let the town be
incorporated, and let town marshals be hired to calm the
fevers of the Texas cowboys.

In September, 1869, the thing was done. Five trustees
were appointed to administer the infant corporation: Mc-
Coy was one of them, and Henry was elected their chair-
man. But who was to pin on the marshal's star? One of
the commissioners, a grocer named Tom Sherran (or
Shearan, or Sheran), was drafted but, when the herds of
cattle were driven north by the cowboys in the spring of
1870, he promptly resigned. One may assume that he was
motivated by the pressure of business in his grocery store.

A pair of anonymous heroes held the job as marshal
conjointly for one day, but they fled after a glimpse of how
the Texans reacted to the notion of town ordinances.
(Copies of an ordinance forbidding the carrying of fire-
arms, having been posted by the trustees, were at once
ripped down or shot to bits.) Henry hopefully wired to St.
Louis for another pair of policemen. The two came, looked
around apprehensively, and went back home on the night
train.

Was Abilene in truth such a tough and lawless town?
The citizens of Detroit, a town about four miles east of
Abilene, certainly thought so: earlier in the year they had

mounted a furious agitation to remove the county seat from Abilene to Detroit. They had charged that Abilene was a seething cauldron of vice and depravity, administered by whores and murderers. As part of their campaign they published a short-lived newspaper which carried a sensational description of the shameless crimes that had made Abilene a hissing and a byword. "In the last three years [1867–1869]," this article ran, "there have been murdered in Abilene 17 men, seven of these were ruthlessly murdered through the influence of fancy women, and six were slaughtered through intemperance and drunken rows, and the remaining four were murdered outright in cruel hand to hand fights. . . . Last summer there were three houses of ill fame and twenty-one fallen women resided in Abilene; . . . there were seventeen saloons. . . ."

While this account does not suggest that Abilene was exactly comatose, on the other hand, if this was the worst that could be said about it by a resentful and jealous neighbor, the town could not have been too rambunctious, especially in view of the fact that it was growing rapidly. (The U.S. census, taken in July, 1870, showed a resident population of between seven and eight hundred persons. A two-story brick courthouse was going up; there was a second church, a second bank, a weekly newspaper, two new hotels, and the beginnings of a new residential neighborhood north of the tracks.) One might reasonably conclude that the violent deaths had come only to those who had chosen to live recklessly—that is to say, to the cowboys—and that those who minded their own business and drank their own whiskey could have found Abilene a tolerably peaceful town.

In that testing spring of 1870, however, the Texans were more ebullient and explosive than ever. They were sullen when they found that the trustees of the town had, by ukase of May 20, obliged the prostitutes to move northwest to some shanties alongside Mud Creek, outside the limits of Abilene. The construction of a town jail was another provocation; they tore it down. When it was rebuilt, under guard, and a first miscreant lodged within it, a gang of them took on a load of the raw white tanglefoot available in the local saloons, converged upon the jail, smashed down its locked doors, and freed the prisoner. To accent their displeasure, as they galloped past Henry's real-estate office they peppered it with a fusillade of bullets.

In his despair, Henry sent a telegram to a man whom the trustees had already once rejected, as like as not because they were too cheap. This was Tom Smith, a husky,

squarefisted man of thirty, born in New York City of Irish parents. As a youngster, Smith had been a skillful prize-fighter, and he had later earned a reputation as a good cop, tough, fair, honest, and ready for anything. He took his oath as the marshal of Abilene on a Saturday morning, June 4, 1870. Within approximately twenty-four hours, Smith had demonstrated that one reasonably mettlesome

Abilene offered
many recreations for a cowhand

peace officer could effectively quell any number of unruly cowboys by the simple expedient of using his bare fists on the most recalcitrant of them. Smith had to use his fists only twice—once on Saturday night and then on Sunday morning—to teach his lesson. Thereafter the cowboys parked their guns with the bartender of the saloon of their choice. Their quarrels were quieter and not so bloody; likewise the town. Abilene was tame.

Tom Smith was, no doubt about it, a blessing to Abilene. Imagine: a peace officer in the Wild, Wild West who neither drank nor gambled, who never used profanity or obscenity, who never killed to keep the peace. No wonder Abilene's trustees gratefully raised his salary from one hundred and fifty dollars a month to two hundred and twenty-five dollars a month (plus half the fines collected, after conviction). These handsome fees were well deserved, for during his tenure some three hundred thousand head of cattle were trailed into Abilene, sold, and hauled out in stockcars; the town grew rich, and all was relatively serene.

During that same year, however, the symbolic Cain-Abel feud was quietly building to a climax. As the representative of the cattle trade, Joe McCoy was in sore trouble. The Kansas Pacific had renounced its agreement with him; thus plunging him in costly litigation to win his rights. He was obliged to sell first his stockyards and then the Drover's Cottage; it seemed that he might even have to part with his own home. Meantime, quite secretly, his ancient friend T. C. Henry had, by a truly seminal experiment, become the representative of the homesteaders, the would-be farmers, those who pinned their hopes on agriculture. Late in 1870 Henry had tilled five acres of the rich bottom-land of the Smoky Hill River and planted them with seed from the winter wheat grown in Minnesota. One reason for his secrecy was that Henry knew he would surely be a laughing-stock if word of his experiment got out, for everybody had long since decided that the soil of central Kansas was good for nothing but cheap pasture. But Henry had been studying the matter. He calculated that if he could prove winter wheat to be a profitable crop he would be, as land agent for the prairies roundabout Abilene, an assured

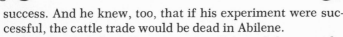
success. And he knew, too, that if his experiment were successful, the cattle trade would be dead in Abilene.

Tom Smith did not live to see the climax of the struggle. On November 2, 1870, Smith was slain—not by the Texans who had come to respect him, but by a good-for-nothing homesteader, who lived in a dugout carved in a hillside a few miles northeast of the town, a man whom Smith had undertaken to arrest on some unimportant charge. The whole town grieved, and most of its people followed Smith's hearse and his riderless horse, Silverheels, to his burying ground.

In the early spring of 1871, with prospects for the cattle trade never brighter, Abilene was busting its britches. Its increase of population authorized the town to claim the proud status of a third-class city, with its own elected mayor. In March, Joe McCoy won a judgment in the District Court against the Kansas Pacific Railroad Company. Flushed with his victory, he ran for mayor and won the election on April 3. (T. C. Henry, who had declined to run, was watching the little green tops of his wheat, as they burst up from his bottomland.)

All around the town, in early April, there were herds of longhorns. They covered every acre of pasture land, for every drover was anxious to sell at the earliest and best price. The Drover's Cottage was jammed with cattlemen, commission agents, cattle buyers, representatives of the big Chicago butchers. The line of saloons and gambling houses and dance halls, just south of the railroad tracks, was ablaze with lights every night. The whores, in town in greater numbers than ever, were soon to be sequestrated in an area southeast of and beyond the town limits (not far from where Dwight David Eisenhower and his brothers, as growing boys, would do their chores and play their games, a little more than twenty years later), in a section called first Texas Town, then the Devil's Half Acre, and finally Fisher's Addition. But nevertheless more cowboys than ever spilled into the town, intimidating the proper citizenry, gambling, carousing, brawling, and generally making a nuisance of themselves.

Clearly, someone was needed to replace Tom Smith, to maintain some semblance of law and order, to ride herd on

the obstreperous cowhands. Someone was needed whose reputation alone would make prospective malefactors quake like jelly on a plate. Who but Wild Bill Hickok? Whose reputation was conceivably more sinister?

And so we return to the all-purpose hero, to the instant,

Gambling was very popular

ready-made, fresh-frozen legend, suitable for consumption with a minimum of effort, the Pablum Kid. *Harper's Monthly* had published, not long before, a lurid account of Hickok's fatal skill in battle, as told to George Ward Nichols by Wild Bill himself. There was, for instance, Hickok's version of the McCanles affair. In truth, Hickok

Cowhands made a nuisance of themselves at times

had shot Dave McCanles down from behind a curtain, shot a second man from behind a door, and mortally wounded a third man as he ran for his life. But as Wild Bill told the tale to Nichols, while the writer's eyes bugged out so far they could have been knocked off with a board, he had been attacked by McCanles and a gang of nine "desperadoes, horse-thieves, murderers, regular cutthroats." He had slain six men with six shots and dispatched the other four "blood-thirsty devils" with his knife.

A man whose fame rested on such fabulous fibs was just the sort needed to quell the frequent riots of a wicked cowtown. At least, so thought Mayor McCoy. Moreover, McCoy knew right where to find his man, for Hickok was already in Abilene, gambling for a living at the Alamo. Wild Bill took the job.

He slung two six-guns from his hips; he thrust a knife in the red sash he affected; he cradled a sawed-off shotgun in his arms. In this fashion, he occasionally patrolled the streets. But only occasionally. Most hours of most evenings he could be found at the Alamo, gambling with the cowboys. (After all, his salary was only one hundred and fifty dollars a month and half the fines collected in court, and why go to the trouble of collecting a fine when the same result can be brought about in a comfortable chair at a gaming table?) Most hours of most nights he had business in Abilene's red-light district, locally called the "Hell Hole of Women." C. F. Gross, who was the clerk at the Drover's Cottage in 1871, and who has been described as one of Wild Bill's most intimate friends, wrote in 1925:

. . . He always had a Mistress I Knew two or three of them, one a former Mistress of his was an inmate of a cottage in McCoys addition. Bill asked me to go with him to see her to be a witness in an interview. I believe she was a Red Head but am not sure. She came to Abilene to try & make up with Bill. He gave her $25.00, & made her move on. There was Nan Ross but Bill told her he was through with her. She moved on. When Mrs Lake the Widow of "Old Lake of Circus fame," Came to Abilene she set up her tent Just West of the D[rover's] Cottage on the vacant ground Bill was on hand to Keep order. Bill was a Handsome man as you Know & she fell for him hard, fell all the way *clear to the Basement,* tried her best to get him to marry her & run the Circus Bill told me all about it. I said why dont you do it—He said "I Know she has a good show, but when she is done in the West, she will go East & I dont want any paper collar on, & its me for the West. . . ."

Meantime the taxpayers of Abilene chafed. Nor were the Texans happy; for they were persuaded that Hickok wore the star only to protect the extortions of the professional gamblers, madames, and saloon keepers.

Matters came to a head on the night of October 5. A bunch of cowboys had been hurrahing the town in their traditional and tiresome fashion—forcing clothing mer-

His skill
was reputed to be fatal

chants to outfit poorly clad strangers, obliging passersby to stand drinks for all hands—and Hickok reportedly had warned them to quiet down. Back in the Alamo at his poker table, Wild Bill heard someone fire a shot. He plunged out into the darkness to confront a Texan named Phil Coe. Some say that Coe's gun was already back in its holster; some that it was dangling in his hand. Whichever the case, Hickok fired, felling Coe, and then, when he heard some-

Wild Bill was known
to enjoy a leisurely card game

one running toward him, at once wheeled and plugged his own deputy, one Mike Williams, in a typical exhibition of coolness, calm, and nerve. He was relieved of his official duties six weeks later.

After that there was nothing left but to let show business exploit his celebrity. He joined Buffalo Bill Cody's stock company, an ignoble engagement, but quit before long. In March, 1876, Mrs. Lake ran across him again in Chey-

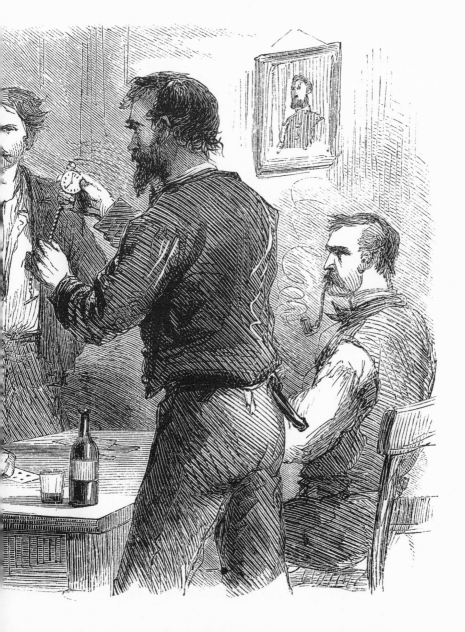

enne; this time she nabbed him and married him. The marriage would not seem to have been all cream-and-honey. In June, a Kansas newspaper reported, from Fort Laramie, that Wild Bill "was arrested on several occasions as a vagrant, having no visible means of support."

Later that month he galloped into Deadwood with a retinue that included, of all people, Calamity Jane. He settled down to gambling, as was his wont; she to drinking, as was hers. A little more than a month passed, and then Jack McCall shot him from behind, for no particular reason.

Hickok had been a brave army scout in the Civil War and against the Indians; he had also been a liar, a fornicator, a professional gambler, and a killer. His score, according to a conservative chronicler of his deeds, was thirty-six men killed, apart from his service in the army and against the Indians. What more fitting, for such a man, than to enshrine him on television, during the children's hour?

There is a tale that tells how Calamity Jane, furious when she hears of Wild Bill's death, pursues his killer and corners him in a butcher shop, where she has to be restrained from splitting his brisket with a cleaver. Alas! not true. There is another tale that tells of how Calamity, on her deathbed years later, whispers, "What's the date?" When she is told it is August 2, she smiles and murmurs, "It's the twenty-seventh anniversary of Bill's death." Then, while the violins sob a little in the background, she adds, "Bury me next to Bill." Alas! this is likewise horsefeathers. She died on August 1, 1903. Yet the legends persist in linking the two together.

Were they lovers? Wild Bill's adherents flatly deny it, claiming that their man was far too fastidious. What their denial lacks in gallantry, it makes up in logic. Calamity was the most celebrated female of the Wild, Wild West, but she was no rose.

She may have been born in 1845 (or 1852), in Missouri (or Illinois); her name may have been Mary Jane Canary (or Conarray). Her mother may have been a prostitute, and may have been a madame in Blackfoot, Montana around 1866, managing a house that may have been called the Bird Cage. Notable citizens of the Wild, Wild West share an irritating nebulosity when it comes to recorded data.

There are seven different theories as to how she came by her name, none of them plausible enough to concern us here. She appears to have got around enough for at least three women. Contemporary newspapers credit her with being all over the West, sometimes all at once.*

This much is certain: Calamity Jane loved the company of men and, as time went on, she craved booze more and more.

Assuming that she was born in 1845, she was twenty when she bobbed up in Montana, conjecturally an orphan; twenty-four when, wearing men's clothes, she was consorting with the railroad section gangs in Piedmont and Cheyenne, Wyoming; twenty-seven when, in Dodge City, she made a cowboy crooner called Darling Bob Mackay dance tenderfoot (i.e., obliged him to scamper about by firing bullets at his feet) because he had said something indelicate about her underwear; thirty when, the only woman, she joined a geological expedition into the Black Hills; and thirty-one when, the only woman amongst fifteen hundred men, she left Fort Laramie with a bull train hauling supplies for General Crook's expedition against the Sioux. Soon after, a scandalized colonel caught her swimming naked with some of her buddies in Hat Creek, near Sheridan, and promptly banished her. Undaunted, she got Grouard, Crook's chief of scouts, to appoint her an Indian scout under his command—or so it was said, but never proved.

By then the unfortunate woman was a seriously sick alcoholic, ready for any man's exploitation if only she could get a drink. Greedy showmen hired her for appearances in dime museums; her ghost-written memoirs were published in a cheap pamphlet, and Calamity took to hawking copies for whatever she could get. There were

* Her confusing ubiquity has been explained by a South Dakota newspaperman, Leonard Jennewein. After careful investigation, he established that there were three Calamity Janes. One, a whore like her more celebrated namesake, was named Mattie Young and died in August, 1878, in Colorado.

Calamity Jane—the most celebrated female was no rose

stories that she had been married twelve times and widowed eleven, but no record exists of her marriage to anybody.

And then, long after Calamity was dead, a woman appeared who produced a paper certifying the marriage on September 1, 1870, of Martha Jane Cannary and James Butler Hickok, and who claimed to be the daughter of Wild Bill and Calamity Jane. She claimed it right out loud, to an audience of several million persons, over a network of radio stations. But presently the document was characterized as a forgery by experts and the chroniclers of the Wild, Wild West could return to their speculations. Perhaps Calamity had been a female hermaphrodite? In that case, how could she possibly have had an affair with Wild Bill? And yet, Wild Bill's appearance was suspiciously effeminate: perhaps he was a male hermaphrodite, in which case, maybe, after all . . . ?

And here let us leave them.

For we have come to our third Horrible—a slope-shouldered man whose blue eyes blink incessantly (he has granulated eyelids), and whose short whiskers grow dark on his chin and lower lip. We are now in the presence of the bandit-hero. He is labeled

  **JAMES**

Jesse, son of Zerelda and Robert

CHAPTER 4

JESSE JAMES

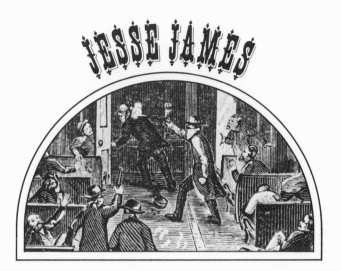

Any study of Jesse Woodson James (September 5, 1847–April 3, 1882), the celebrated Missouri ruffian, murderer, bank robber, train robber, and American demi-god, is best prefaced by a quick glimpse at his mother, Zerelda E. Cole James Simms Samuel. She was, by all accounts, a notable woman.

After attending a Roman Catholic convent school in Lexington, Kentucky, she married a Baptist seminarian, Robert James. He left her to seek gold in California, where he died. After her second husband died as she was about to divorce him, she married a third, "a meek man." "She was, all her life, a religious woman," says one of Jesse's admiring biographers. "Love became her religion," says another. But there was her temper to contend with: "It was hot and fiery." Moreover, like a battleship of the line, she had plenty to back her temper with: "She was six feet tall," said a proud grandson, "and weighed two hundred twenty-eight pounds." However, the first biographer reminds us: "She was a woman thoroughly good and noble." Most certainly, the second agrees; and then informs us that, after her notorious son had been killed, she "boldly" showed tourists around Jesse's old farm, "extracting every dime she could from them." "This woman who had always been so upright," he adds, sold the tourists stones allegedly from Jesse's grave but actually from the creek. She also sold tourists enough shoes from the horses her two bandit sons had ridden "to fill a wagonbed."

But hear her cry out at Jesse's funeral, whilst two ministers lead the mourners in singing "We Will Wait Till Jesus Comes."* "Oh, my generous, noble-hearted Jesse," she moans, clearly enough to be heard by the reporters attending. "Oh, why did they kill my poor boy who never wronged anybody, but helped them and fed them with the bread that should go to his orphans?"

Her poor, generous, noble-hearted boy, who never wronged anybody, was the leader of a gang of comparably generous, noble-hearted thugs who, in fifteen years, held up eleven banks, seven trains, three stages, one county fair, and one payroll messenger, in the process looting some two hundred thousand dollars and killing at least sixteen men. What the mothers of these sixteen said at their graves has not been recorded.

Jesse's deification was confected according to the classic recipe of the *Police Gazette*—his prankish charm, his courteous behavior to women involved in his stick-ups, his protection of fictitious widows from villainous bankers seeking to foreclose fictitious mortgages, and all the rest— but in his case a unique attribute was added, one guaranteed to inflame the partisan passions bred of the Civil War.

---

* Or, as it may have been, "What a Friend We Have in Jesus." As seems always to be the case in these histories of Wild, Wild West personages, the authorities cannot agree on anything, no matter how grave of import.

For Jesse symbolized the gallant rebel ground down beneath the boot of the victorious Yankee oppressor, and such was the potency of this bogus magic that he actually kept a sovereign state in an uproar for an entire decade. When at last he died, shot in the back by a man allegedly deputized to do the job by the governor of Missouri, one of the state's most respected newspaper editors called for the assassination of the public officials involved, and cried out:

Tear the two bears from the flag of Missouri! Put thereon, in place of them, as more appropriate, a thief blowing out the brains of an unarmed victim, and a brazen harlot, naked to the waist and splashed to the brows in blood!

The thief was Bob Ford; the harlot was Mattie Collins, the concubine of Dick Liddil (this name is spelled in at least four different ways), who was also the woman who engineered the turning of state's evidence by Liddil against James; the unarmed victim was, of course, Jesse himself; but the threnodial wrath was the unspent passion of the Gray against the Blue.

Jesse grew up in an atmosphere of hate. Missouri men rode across the line into Kansas to cast the fraudulent votes they hoped would make Kansas a slave state; Kansas men resisted; Missouri men rode again to raid and kill; Kansas men rode back in vengeance. When the Civil War erupted, there was a whole generation of teen-age toughs living in the tier of Missouri counties that border on Kansas, all of them handy with guns and knives, all of them committed on the political issues of the day, all of them itching to start a rumble. To name just a handful of these hellions:

Up in Clay County there were Frank James, eighteen, and his brother Jesse, fourteen, of whom later the ballad would sing: He was born one day in the County of Clay/ And he came from a solitary race."

Just south, on a farm in Jackson County, there were Cole Younger, seventeen, Jim Younger, thirteen, and two other brothers, Bob and John, who were still just children. (Across another county line, in Cass County, there lived the Daltons, close kin to the Youngers; but their brood,

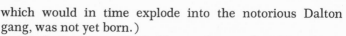

which would in time explode into the notorious Dalton gang, was not yet born.)

A little further south, in Vernon County, lived Jim Reed, sixteen.

And still further south, in Jasper County, there were Ed Shirley, about eighteen, and his sister, Myra Belle, thirteen.

All these youngsters (except Myra Belle) became bushwhackers, i.e., Confederate irregulars, most of them serving under the infamous William C. Quantrill, the psychopathic turncoat and killer who is justifiably remembered as "the bloodiest man known in the annals of America." Frank James and Cole Younger were with Quantrill when, in August, 1863, the town of Lawrence, Kansas, was sacked and one hundred and eighty-two of its citizens murdered. Jesse James and Jim Younger were with Quantrill's lieutenant, Bloody Bill Anderson, at the Centralia massacre a year later, when more than two hundred Federal soldiers were shot down, many of them being prisoners. Jesse is credited with killing the commander, Major H. J. Johnson. Jesse was then seventeen.

With the end of the war, most of the bushwhackers laid down their guns and went to work as decent citizens. Not, however, this handful. The James and Younger brothers (and probably Jim Reed) hitched together a gang of likeminded hooligans who went right on robbing and killing. Their first score, at Liberty, Missouri, on February 13, 1866, was against the Clay County Savings Association Bank, an institution where, it may be presumed, many of their friends and neighbors kept their money. They stole sixty-two thousand dollars and killed one man. Why should they turn back, after such a success?

In between robberies and murders, they occupied themselves variously. When Cole Younger, for example, hid out in Texas in 1868, who should he find down there near Dallas but li'l ole Myra Belle Shirley! Why, the last time he saw Myra Belle, back in Jasper County, she was just a scrawny kid in pigtails! But before long she was the mother of his bastard, a girl she named Pearl Younger. And when Jim Reed came south in 1870, also on the lam, Myra Belle took him also into her house, and she cleaved unto him and presented him also with a bastard, a boy she

The James brothers profited from wartime lessons

Jesse did not always keep holy the Sabbath Day

named Ed Reed. For his part, Jim Younger whiled away the time between robberies by serving as a deputy sheriff in Dallas.

But the acknowledged leader of "The Boys," as they were fondly called, had no use for such tomfoolery because, we are told, he was too pious. Jesse James was baptized and added to the strength of the Kearney Baptist Church near his home in 1868 (soon after he had killed a man in a bank robbery at Richmond, Missouri). He sang in church choirs; he even organized a group of the faithful and taught hymn-singing (a few months after murdering the cashier of a bank in Gallatin, Missouri). His Bible, we are assured, was well-thumbed; but apparently he skipped the chapters in Exodus where the Ten Commandments are listed, for he continued to kill and to steal, and at least twice he did not remember the Sabbath day, to keep it holy, but rather used it as the occasion for a train robbery.

By 1874 Jesse's crimes were a chief issue in Missouri's gubernatorial campaign: whether or not to suppress outlawry so that "capital and immigration can once again enter our state." But nothing was done; his raids continued.

By 1881 the baying was so close at Jesse's heels that, pious or no, he likewise took off for Myra Belle's recherché resort for the criminally inclined. She had removed to a country place on the Canadian River in Oklahoma, which for nostalgic reasons she called Younger's Bend. Belle, having by now given the boot to such sometime outlaw-lovers as Jack Spaniard, Jim French, Jim July, John Middleton, and the white man who incomprehensibly chose to be called Blue Duck, had actually got married, to a Cherokee named Sam Starr. Consequently, she was now known as Belle Starr. If Jesse could have known that she would one day be celebrated all over the country as the Bandit Queen, or, the Female Jesse James, he might have cursed a tiny curse, pious man that he may have been notwithstanding. But he was dead before that remarkable day. And now it is time to toll out the necrology of the teen-age hellions listed above:

Frank James died in 1915, at seventy-two. "He never was," wrote a doting reporter for the *St. Louis Republic*, "a

Belle Starr and friend Blue Duck

criminal at heart. . . . His intelligence was of a high order, very far above the average. . . ."

Jesse James was shot in the back of the head in 1882, at thirty-five, by "the dirty little coward" Bob Ford.

Cole Younger died at his home in Missouri in 1916, at seventy-two, "a good man," according to the obituary in his local newspaper. He had been wounded twenty-six times, but nine bullets had torn clear through him. He took seventeen slugs to his grave. He had served twenty-five years in jail.

Jim Younger, who also served twenty-five years in jail (he and his brother had been caught by some outraged citizens of Minnesota after trying to hold up the Northfield bank), shot himself in 1902 when the parents of a girl he had hoped to marry refused their permission. He was fifty-four.

Bob Younger, captured in Minnesota, died in jail of tuberculosis, in 1889. He was in his thirties.

John Younger was shot to death by Pinkerton officers, at the age of twenty-four.

Jim Reed was shot and killed from behind, by John T. Morris, a deputy sheriff of Collin County, Texas, on August 6, 1874. Morris, the killer, had formerly been Jim Reed's confederate in stagecoach robberies and the theft of livestock.

Ed Shirley was killed by Federal soldiers when he was about twenty.

Myra Belle Shirley, horse thief, cattle thief, suspected robber of stagecoaches, constant concubine of and protector of desperate criminals, was shot in the back and killed near Eufaula, Oklahoma, on February 3, 1889. A neighbor, Edgar Watson, was accused of her murder but the charges against him were dismissed. She was probably slain by her son, Ed Reed, with whom she had had incestuous relations. He was angry with his mother, for she had whipped him after he rode her favorite horse without her permission. So it went, out in the glamorous, romantic Wild, Wild West. Scarcely a day passed without some gay and gallant gunslinger shooting his way into the affections of future generations. We have just time to tell how *The National Police Gazette* described the girl who was born Myra Belle Shirley:

Their deeds immortalized those gallant gunslingers

—Of all women of the Cleopatra type, since the days of the Egyptian queen herself, the universe has produced none more remarkable than Bella Starr, the Bandit Queen. . . . She was more amorous than Anthony's mistress, more relentless than Pharaoh's daughter, and braver than Joan of Arc. Of her it may well be said that Mother Nature was indulging in one of her rarest freaks, when she produced such a novel specimen of womankind . . . well-educated, . . . gifted with uncommon musical and literary talents . . . In a strange country, and under an assumed name, she brightened the social circle for a week or a month, and then was, perhaps, lost forever.

Her son was convicted of bootlegging in the Indian Territory and sent to a Federal penitentiary in 1891. Pardoned two years later, he was appointed a deputy marshal in Fort Smith, killed two men who were hurrahing a town in Oklahoma, and was himself killed in 1896 while shooting up a saloon.

Belle's daughter, Pearl Younger, appeared in a vaudeville show in Dallas, at her mother's insistence, when she was fourteen. She collapsed on the stage. Two years after her mother's death, Pearl was a whore in Fort Smith. A few months later she opened her own bagnio.

There is a statue of Belle in Ponca City, Oklahoma. There she stands in bronze, her gaze clear-eyed, her Winchester leveled, her six-gun hanging in a cartridge belt, ready, by her right hand; noble, idealized, the apotheosis of the Frontier Woman—a brazen lie and a brazen horse-laugh.

Her old neighbor Jesse James lies under a monument near the site of the Kearney Baptist Church. The inscription reads:

In Loving Remembrance of My Beloved Son

JESSE JAMES

Died April 3, 1882

AGED 34 YEARS, 6 MONTHS, 28 DAYS

MURDERED BY A TRAITOR AND COWARD WHOSE

NAME IS NOT WORTHY TO APPEAR HERE.

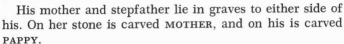

His mother and stepfather lie in graves to either side of his. On her stone is carved MOTHER, and on his is carved PAPPY.

But had Jesse really been murdered in 1882? There were folk in Clay County—and elsewhere, too—who whispered that the murder had been staged, that Jesse still lived and would ride again. He *couldn't* have died: he was too sorely needed as a surrogate for the outlaw that hides inside us all. The flood of dime novels about him, the plays, the six motion pictures contrived by Hollywood were not enough: the gullible still swore that Jesse lived. Naturally, this being the case, men claiming to be Jesse began to appear one after another. It was good business, if they weren't greedy and didn't appear too closely on each other's heels, for each claimant could make money from his memoirs and from appearances in vaudeville or on radio programs. But at length time ran out on them. The last claimant bobbed up in 1948, which meant that he had to act one hundred and one years old, an irksome role. This scalawag at least had the wit to take an appropriate alias. He asserted that he had lived through the years as Frank Dalton, a name which, since it recalled the Dalton gang of the 1890s, fitly closed the circle of Wild West outlawry.

Perhaps it will be a relief to turn to our next exhibit. This time we have two men mounted on the same pedestal, standing shoulder to shoulder; pals, pards till hell freezes. Each is expressionless, poker-faced; each has hard blue-gray eyes and affects a handlebar moustache; each wears black broadcloth and white linen, and a star; at each hip hangs a six-gun. Clearly we are now confronting the men who tamed the Wild, Wild West. Sure enough, for their labels read

 EARP and MASTERSON

Dodge City, 1878

CHAPTER 5

WYATT EARP AND

BAT MASTERSON

As we approach Wyatt Earp and Bat Masterson, and eye their papier-mâché figures somewhat dubiously, it would be well for us to check our supply of gullibility, for we shall need plenty of it if we are to take these two seriously. The flimflam that has been confected about this pair, and especially about Earp, has developed over the last forty years into a most profitable cottage industry, bringing gainful employment to biographers, novelists, and comic-book artists, and more particularly to the writers, actors, and technicians who toil in the cloaca maxima of television. So beguiling has their flimflam been, that it has taken on the aura of scripture, of revealed truth.

Are halos visible above the heads of our two heroes?

Not always, for they sometimes wear high-crown brown bowlers with curly rims, the kind that in their time would have been worn by hotel detectives, or by respectable bartenders heading for a picnic on their day off, or by—now we are getting closer to the truth—professional gamblers. Can it be? It seems so far from what we have always been told of these two.

Earp and Masterson were two of the regnant superheroes of the televised Wild West. Once upon a time they faced the same foes in the same filmed fables, but times changed; they went their separate sponsored ways. This is a pity, for in real life the two were as thick as thieves.

Each week we were shown, in bland, bright little slices of televised entertainment, just how they scrubbed the West clean, including the back of its neck and behind its ears. Clean-cut and clean-shaven, Wyatt romanced Nellie Cashman, the "miners' angel," or he avenged the murder of some Indian friends, or he trapped some mining executives who would thieve silver bullion. Elegant and clean-shaven, Bat foiled a horse-race swindler, or he gallantly assisted some ladies in their struggle for women's rights, or by examining the brushwork he perceived that some oil paintings were spurious. All this was only so much ingenious fretwork on the Earp-Masterson legend, contrived by worthy successors to the staffwriters of *The National Police Gazette*. But the legend is itself such an imposing structure as to require no further embellishment.

The legend tells us that Marshal Earp cleaned up two Kansas cowtowns, Ellsworth and Wichita, single-handed. He then joined forces with Bat Masterson to clean up Dodge City, the "Gomorrah of the plains," "the wickedest little city in America," "the bibulous Babylon of the frontier." So much accomplished, Marshal Earp turned his attention to the featherweight task of pacifying Tombstone, Arizona, a hotbed of outlaws unparalleled in history, whilst Sheriff Masterson proceeded to stamp out sin in the mining camps of Colorado. Thereafter both men retired, breathing easily, having made the Wild, Wild West safe for the effete tenderfeet of the East.

Both men, the legend adds, were courteous to women, modest, handsome, and blue-eyed. We are also told that Earp was the West's speediest and deadliest gunfighter. For his part, Masterson disdained to pull a gun, preferring to clout an adversary senseless with his cane, whence his nickname. But he was quite willing to testify to his pal's prowess, and so contribute to the legend. Earp could, Masterson has assured us, kill a coyote with his Colt .45 at four hundred yards.* He added: "Offhand, I could list fifty gunfights in which Wyatt put a slug through the arm or the shoulder of some man who was shooting at him, when he might as certainly have shot him in the belly or through the heart . . . Where human life was concerned, Wyatt was the softest-hearted gunfighter I knew. Yet, if circumstances demanded, he could kill more swiftly and more surely than any other man of record in his time."

This is an odd testimonial, for in Earp's hagiography only one killing by him is reported that Masterson could possibly have witnessed. Masterson himself, who was in truth a poor shot, killed at most four men throughout his career (not counting Indians). Indeed, these two differ sharply from other Wild, Wild West heroes in that they rarely fired their six-guns in anger. They were both sly, cunning, cautious men, who learned early that shooting might reap a bloody harvest. In consequence, they walked warily, carrying a big bluff. In their time, the killer and outlaw was dying out, to be replaced by the confidence man. Confidence men rarely kill; they are too artful. Both Earp and Masterson were, among other things, eager students of the technique of early confidence games.

They first met in 1872, when both were hunting buffalo

---

* Such skill calls for some respectful analysis. At four hundred yards a coyote cannot be seen against his natural background, so we shall assume the animal is silhouetted against the sky. Even so, an expert using a rifle with a globe sight would congratulate himself if he hit such a target with any regularity, much more if he killed it. A pistol of course will not carry so far when aimed directly; the marksman must use Kentucky windage, i.e., he must aim appreciably above his target so that his bullet will carry. Masterson admitted that "luck figures largely in such shooting." If, instead of "largely," he had said "completely," he would have come closer to that coyote.

on the Salt Fork of the Arkansas, in direct violation of the Indian treaty. Earp was twenty-four; Masterson was nineteen. They seem to have recognized that they were kindred souls, but they parted, not to come together again until the summer of 1876, in Dodge City. During those four years, Bat was, so to say, preparing himself to be a peace officer. He stole forty ponies from some Indians and sold them for twelve hundred dollars, he killed Indians both as a freelance buffalo hunter and as an army scout, and he got into a brawl with an army sergeant at Sweetwater, Texas, over a dancehall girl. The girl was killed while trying to shield Masterson; Bat was wounded, but he killed the soldier.

Meantime Earp, by his own account, had engaged in even more impressive heroics. First there was his mettlesome exploit at Ellsworth in 1873. To hear him tell it, Earp stepped out of a crowd, unknown and unheralded, and stalked alone across that familiar sunbaked plaza to disarm an able and truculent gunfighter, the Texas gambler Ben Thompson. Not only that, but Thompson was backed up at the time by a hundred pugnacious cowboy friends. How could Earp ever have dared to do it? He would seem to have been cloaked in invisibility, for others who were present never saw him—not the reporter for the Ellsworth newspaper; not Thompson himself; not Deputy Sheriff Hogue, to whom Thompson voluntarily turned over his gun; and not Mayor James Miller, to whom Thompson gave bond for his appearance when he might be wanted later. Is it possible Earp was telling a great big fib?

In May, 1874, Earp arrived in Wichita, another rowdy cowtown, where, he said later, Mayor Jim Hope promptly made him the marshal. Let Earp speak: "In two years at Wichita my deputies and I arrested more than eight hundred men. In all that time I had to shoot but one man— and that only to disarm him. All he got was a flesh wound."

And now a look at the minutes of the Wichita city commission. They show that Earp was elected on April 21, 1875, as one of two policemen to serve under the marshal and assistant marshal. They show further that on April 19, 1876, the commission voted against rehiring him. A month later it was recommended that the vagrancy act be enforced against Earp and his brother Jim.

Earp was a man of reputation in Ellsworth and Witchita

Judging from the Wichita newspapers, Earp seems not to have won much of a reputation during his one year as a policeman. They keep referring to him as "Policeman Erp," which makes him sound like a sandwich man for Dr. Brown's Celery Tonic. Now and then he arrested a suspected horse thief; but the longest newspaper story about him describes how he was arrested, fined, and fired from the police force for violating the peace on April 5, 1876. All this resulted from an election-eve fracas in which Earp slugged an opposition candidate for city marshal. The reporter concluded: "It is but justice to Erp to say he has made an excellent officer, and hitherto his conduct has been unexceptionable."

But it was time he was moving on, and so he turned up in Dodge City.

In 1876 Dodge had one major source of income: cattle. The gangs who built the railroad had disappeared; the hunters of bison had dwindled away; the only men with outside money were the Texas cattle owners and the cowpokes who worked for them. The town's fathers, then, had only one problem: how, without being too crude, to separate these Texans from their money during the few months—June through September—when they would be in town? Liquor, women, and games of chance; these seemed the likeliest solutions to the problem, and their supply led naturally to the way in which the town was administered.

Dodge was run by a small clique of saloonkeepers who, as the years went on, took turns being mayor. Most saloons were routinely outfitted with gambling layouts. In 1878 the town council enacted an ordinance against gambling. Had its members gone out of their minds? No: they were moved by sound common sense. For, with a law on the books prohibiting gambling, any chump who complained that he had been cheated could be forthwith walked Spanish to the hoosegow on the grounds that he had been breaking the law.

A town run along these lines clearly required something special in the way of a peace officer: a man who would know how and when to enforce the freakish laws, who would know how to wink at the artful ways in which visitors from Texas were mulcted. We are told that the saloonkeeper who was mayor in 1876, one George Hoover, sent for Wyatt Earp. Let Earp speak again: "The message that took me to Dodge had offered me the marshal's job, but Hoover told me that for political reasons he wanted [Marshal Larry] Deger to complete his year in office. . . . I would have power to hire and fire deputies . . . and be marshal in all but name . . ." Earp told his skillful biographer, Stuart Lake, that he had appointed two deputies and was looking for a third "when Bat [Masterson] came in from Sweetwater, Texas, still limping from the leg-wound he got when he killed Sergeant King. Bat's gun-hand was in working order, so I made him a deputy. He patrolled Front Street with a walking-stick for several weeks and used his cane to crack the heads of several wild men hunting trouble; even as a cripple he was a first-class peace officer."

Earp also asserted that he was paid two hundred and fifty dollars a month, plus a fee of two dollars and fifty cents for each arrest. He and his deputies, he said, arrested some three hundred persons a month, or enough to bring in about seven hundred and fifty dollars a month. (One month in 1877, he recalled, the fees reached almost one thousand dollars from nearly four hundred arrests; that was the peak.) Earp's share would have brought his income to around four hundred and fifty dollars a month, nice money for the time and place.

And now to the town records. Earp was never marshal of Dodge. He served two terms as assistant marshal: from May 17, 1876 to September 9, 1876, and from May 12, 1878 to September 8, 1879. (During that month of 1877 when, by his own account, he and his deputies arrested nearly four hundred Texans, the *Dodge City Times* reported that a dancehall girl, one "Miss Frankie Bell . . . heaped epithets upon the unoffending head of Mr. Earp to such an extent as to provoke a slap from the ex-officer." Miss Bell was fined twenty dollars the next morning; Mr. Earp was fined a dollar.)

Earp's salary as assistant marshal, as evidenced by bills approved at a meeting of the City Council in August, 1878, was seventy-five dollars. The fee paid for an arrest (and

Run by saloonkeepers,
Dodge required a special peace officer

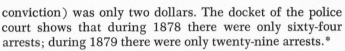

conviction) was only two dollars. The docket of the police court shows that during 1878 there were only sixty-four arrests; during 1879 there were only twenty-nine arrests.*

One interpretation of the remarkable decline of arrests in Dodge—from an alleged three hundred or four hundred a month in 1876–1877 to a documented four a month in 1878–1879—is that Wyatt Earp, lion-hearted and Argus-eyed, had tamed the town. There is another interpretation.

At all events, it is clear that Earp's income in 1878 could not have been much more than eighty dollars a month—not much money for the time and place. Bat Masterson's income was about the same. Both somehow had to add to it. Both did: as professional gamblers.

It has been argued that professional gambling in the Wild, Wild West was honest. The witnesses to this preposterous thesis are, of course, the professional gamblers themselves; but even they are circumspect in their testimony, lest they be struck by lightning. Listen, for example, to Bat Masterson: "Gambling," he said, "was not only the principal and best-paying industry of [Dodge City], but was also reckoned among its most respectable." Since there was little else in Dodge City, save prostitution and the liquor trade, his statement is credible. But to suggest that professional gambling in the West was honest is to impose on credulity. Obviously it was no more honest than professional gambling whenever and wherever—which is to say, no more honest than it had to be.

Earp was a professional gambler long before he got to Dodge; his reputation around Hays City was that of a cardplayer who was "up to some dishonest trick every time he played." Masterson, who left Dodge in July, 1876, to follow the goldrush to Deadwood, in the Dakota Territory, got no further than Cheyenne, Wyoming, where he did so well as a faro banker that he stuck.

But, he figured, the pickings would be easier in Dodge, so he was back for the cattle season of 1877. On the night of June 6, he came upon Marshal Larry Deger, who had

---

* The material in this paragraph is taken from Stanley Vestal's entertaining history of Dodge City, *Queen of Cowtowns.* Mr. Vestal cites no police-court docket for the years 1876–1877.

Masterson understood the industrial complex in Dodge

arrested a miscreant and was escorting him to jail. Bat playfully tackled the marshal, enabling the prisoner to escape. For this hooliganism, Bat was jailed and next morning fined twenty-five dollars and costs. Then he returned to his faro bank.

However, Masterson badly wanted a star. Every professional gambler needed a star; the badge of office permitted its wearer to carry a gun, which in turn provided just the psychological advantage necessary in a game of chance played for high stakes. (Only peace officers were permitted to carry guns in Dodge City; all others were obliged to check their weapons in racks provided for the purpose.) Bat might wangle an appointment as a special policeman in Dodge, but such preferments were capricious; who knew but what some new marshal might not strip him of his badge? And so early in June he decided to seek a more permanent post: he would run for sheriff of Ford County.

Masterson's electioneering technique was simplicity itself: he bought an interest in the Lone Star Dance Hall. Only so could a candidate convince the bizarre electorate of Dodge City that he was a sound citizen and a responsible tax-payer. In November, 1877, Bat was elected by a three-vote margin. He took office in January and, what is more, he started off in high gear. He had been sheriff less than a month when a six-man gang of outlaws held up a train in the next county. Despite the fact that the felony was outside his jurisdiction, Bat led a posse that captured two of the robbers without firing a shot, and not long afterward Bat, his brother Ed, and his deputy collared two more of the robbers near Dodge, again without a fight. In April, when a pair of drunks killed his brother Ed, then Dodge's marshal, Bat shot them both, wounding one mortally.

But as the months wore on, like Earp and like Hickok before him, he whiled away his evening hours as a professional gambler in the company of cronies like Doc Holliday, an alcoholic ex-dentist, and Luke Short, a dandiprat. Earp banked faro at the Long Branch Saloon for a percentage of the house's gross. He and Bat and the others spent so many nights in Dodge's brothels that the Texans nicknamed them "the Fighting Pimps."

There was justification for the slur. Earp was living with a girl called Mattie Blaylock; since no record of any marriage has ever been found, she is presumed to have been his common-law wife. And Nyle Miller, director of the Kansas State Historical Society, has established that, according to the census of 1880, Bat Masterson was living with Annie Ladue, nineteen years old, described as his concubine, whilst his younger brother Jim Masterson, by then Dodge's marshal in his turn, was living with Minnie Roberts, sixteen years old, also a concubine. As Mr. Miller commented acidly: "Maybe that was the way some of the officers in those days kept watch over juvenile delinquents. They just lived with them."

By that time Bat was no longer sheriff, having been walloped in his bid for reelection by George Hinkle, a bartender. Earp had also turned in his star. Dodge was not appreciable tamer, but the silver strike in the Arizona hills meant that there might be more money lying around loose in Tombstone; Earp followed his brother Virgil there in December, 1879. With him came his common-law wife, Mattie; with him too were other Earps, his brothers Jim and Morgan and their wives; and presently, tagging along after him, came Doc Holliday with his wife, Big Nose Kate Fisher, a former Dodge prostitute.

Tombstone, they soon found, was strangely unlike Dodge City. Four churches were going up. (Groton's future headmaster, Endicott Peabody, was the young Episcopalian clergyman.) There were carpets in the saloons, forsooth, and French phrases on the menus in the restaurants. No doubt about it, the Wild, Wild West was running out of steam.

Dogged traditionalists, Wyatt Earp got a job as a shotgun messenger for Wells Fargo and his brother Jim caught on as a faro banker. Before long Wyatt was a civil deputy sheriff of Pima County. (Frank Waters, whose eye-opening book, *The Earp Brothers of Tombstone,* is based on the recollections of Virgil Earp's widow, Allie, says Wyatt got his appointment in settlement of a debt run up in a poker game.) But his tenure was brief, and he was replaced by John Behan. When a new county, Cochise, was carved out of the eastern half of Pima, Earp, as a Republican, fancied that John Charles Frémont, the Republican territorial governor, would surely appoint him sheriff. The job, involving tax collections, was a rich plum. It went to Behan, a Democrat, and Earp scowled.

Wyatt was not, as the legend has it, a United States marshal at this time. His brother Virgil had been appointed a deputy marshal for southern Arizona in November, 1879, and appointed an assistant town marshal of Tombstone in October, 1880; but Wyatt, after his brief term as deputy sheriff of Pima County, went back to gambling at the Oriental Saloon, to be joined before long by Luke Short and Bat Masterson. The "Fighting Pimps" were staging a reunion.

Short and Masterson soon left, to stir up trouble elsewhere; but Earp and Doc Holliday were so deeply involved in a vendetta with some other thieves that, perforce, they had to linger in Tombstone.

A word about Doc Holliday. He was, from every account but Wyatt's, a mean and vicious man. He was Georgia-born, tubercular, and fond of killing. After killing two Negroes in Georgia, he fled to Texas; after killing a man in Dallas, he fled; after killing a soldier near Fort Richardson, he fled; after wounding a man in Denver, he fled. It was the pattern of his life. Then he met Earp. "Doc idolized him," Masterson said later. And Earp, for his part, found much to admire in Holliday.

"Two and three quarts of liquor a day was not unusual for him," Earp told his biographer, Stuart Lake, "yet I never saw him stagger with intoxication.* . . . With all of Doc's shortcomings and his undeniably poor disposition, I found him a loyal friend and good company . . ."

Earp's trouble began on the night of March 15, 1881, when a stagecoach left Tombstone carrying eight passengers and, we are told, eighty thousand dollars' worth of bullion.† Bandits attempted to halt this miracle of trans-

---

* If any further proof were needed that Wyatt Earp was an incorrigible liar and blowhard, we have it here. Physiologists are agreed that a healthy man can metabolize no more than one quart of ninety-five proof liquor in a day.

† It is always instructive to examine Western estimates. At a dollar per fine ounce, eighty thousand dollars' worth of silver bullion would weigh two and one-half tons, a staggering load for the coach, not to mention the six horses.

portation. They failed, but in the process they killed the driver and one passenger. The killer was, according to a statement by his wife, Doc Holliday; and the talk around town was that the brain behind the bungled hold-up was Wyatt Earp's. Moving fast, the Earps persuaded Mrs. Holliday to retract her statement and bundled her out of town lest she contradict the retraction. There remained the task of silencing forever Holliday's accomplices.

Wyatt went to one of their friends, Ike Clanton, and offered a deal. If Clanton would arrange to have those accomplices hold up another stage so that Earp and Holliday could ambush them, he, Earp, would guarantee that Clanton would be paid the reward for their capture. Clanton seems to have considered this offer seriously, but at length he refused. The rebuff was serious, for Ike was a blabbermouth who could not be trusted to keep the offer quiet.

Nor did he. Scared stiff that he would be shot for a stool-pigeon, Clanton denied everything, so loudly and publicly that Doc Holliday overheard him and reported to Wyatt. That was in mid-October. Something would have to be done.

On October 26, Ike Clanton was back in Tombstone with his younger brother, Billy. With them were Frank and Tom McLowry and another youngster, Billy Claiborne. All these men were cattle-rustlers or, at the very least, hard cases. That morning Virgil Earp, as town marshal, deputized his brothers Wyatt and Morgan and thereafter the three prowled the streets, seeking to pick a quarrel with the Clantons or the McLowrys. Virgil Earp clubbed Ike Clanton with the barrel of his revolver. Wyatt Earp deliberately jostled Tom McLowry and then struck him. But despite the provocations, there was no fight.

That afternoon the Clanton brothers, the McLowry brothers, and Claiborne went to the O. K. Corral to pick up their horses and ride out of town. Wyatt, Virgil, and Morgan Earp, together with Doc Holliday, went after them. Sheriff Behan tried to interfere, but he was brushed aside. The Earps and Holliday marched into the corral. Somebody spoke; somebody started shooting. After a couple of minutes, Billy Clanton was dead, Frank and Tom McLowry were dead, whilst Ike Clanton and Billy Claiborne, having run for their lives, were safe. Morgan Earp was hit in the left shoulder; Virgil in the leg.

The Earp worshippers have described these slayings as a triumph of law and order over vicious outlawry. In Tombstone the reaction was somewhat different. A sign over the

The fabled O.K. Corral

caskets of the dead proclaimed: MURDERED IN THE STREETS OF TOMBSTONE. A mining engineer, named Lewis, who had witnessed what he called cold-blooded murder, was one of three men appointed by the Citizens' Safety Committee to tell the Earps that there should be no more killing inside the town's limits, and that, if there were, the Committee would act without regard to law. Finally, Virgil Earp was fired as town marshal on October 29.

At all events, friends of those slain took matters into their own hands. Virgil Earp was ambushed and wounded on December 28. In March, 1882, Morgan Earp was picked off in the middle of a billiards game, by a sharpshooter who fired through a window from an alley in back. By this time Wyatt Earp had at long last been deputized as a Federal marshal. He in turn deputized such gunmen as Doc Holliday, Turkey Creek Jack Johnson, and Texas Jack Vermillion, and took off, so he said, in pursuit of his brother's killers.

He rode and he rode, but he never came back. He rode north and east to Colorado where, he hoped, he would be safe. Behind him he left Mattie, his common-law wife, who had taken in sewing at a penny a yard when money was scarce. Behind him, too, he left a town so far from being tamed that President Chester Arthur was obliged, a few months later, to threaten martial law. It was left to a short-spoken, sawed-off, former Texas ranger named John H. Slaughter to restore order to Cochise County. (Slaughter's eyes were dark brown; he was, despite his name, a color-less, if effective, sheriff. So he has never become a "hero.")

And meanwhile, what of Bat Masterson? He had hustled back to Dodge City from Tombstone in April, 1881, in response to a hurry-up plea for help from his younger brother, Jim. This worthy, still Dodge's marshal and also co-owner of a dancehall, had got into a scrape with his partner, A. J. Peacock, and the man they employed as bartender, Al Updegraff, but was apparently too timid to do his own fighting. His big brother stepped off the train at noon on April 16. Peacock and Updegraff were there waiting and once again the tiresome shooting commenced. It was laughable. They all fired their guns empty, without effect. Some unknown hero, employing a rifle, wounded

Dancehalls were a sound investment in the Wild West

Updegraff from behind. Masterson was fined eight dollars for shooting his pistol on the street. The *Ford County Globe* commented: "The citizens are thoroughly aroused and will not stand any more foolishness," whilst the *Jetmore Republican* referred caustically to "the old gang." Bat and his brother were ordered out of town.

Like a cat, Bat landed on his feet in Trinidad, Colorado, where in addition to running a gambling concession he appears to have been appointed a peace officer. Certainly he had some political influence. For, when an Arizona sheriff came to Denver with a request for the extradition of Wyatt Earp and Doc Holliday, Masterson helped protect them. He got out a warrant for Holliday's arrest on the charge of running a confidence game. This superseded the request for extradition, after which the charges against Holliday were of course dropped. "I know him well," Bat told a reporter from the *Denver Republican,* speaking of Holliday. "He was with me in Dodge, where he was known as an enemy of the lawless element."

But the trail led down from glory. In the 1890s Masterson ran a faro layout at the Arcade in Denver, then notoriously the crookedest town in the country. (Earp was dealing nearby, at the Central.) But around the turn of the century Bat was even ordered to leave Denver—it was like being told he was too low for the sewer. In 1902 he went to New York, where he was at once arrested. On the train from Chicago he had, it seems, fleeced a Mormon elder of sixteen thousand dollars by using marked cards in a faro game. No matter. New York was then also corrupt: Bat was bailed by John Considine, a partner of Big Tim Sullivan, who bossed the town. The elder was persuaded to mumble that he must have been mistaken when he identified Masterson. "The man who had the fastest gun" was put out to pasture as a sports writer for *The Morning Telegraph.*

Meantime Earp had married a San Francisco woman named Josephine Marcus. As late as July, 1911, he was accused of complicity in a confidence game. The ugliest bit of his past has been, with some disgust, dug up by Frank Waters. It concerns Mattie, the girl Earp deserted in Tombstone. Alone and friendless, Mattie drifted first to

Globe and then to a mining camp near Willcox, Arizona. She was reduced to whoring for a living. In July, 1888, she died of an overdose of laudanum, a suicide. The coroner who sent her few effects back to her family in Iowa tucked into the package a letter in which he wrote that Mattie had been deserted by "a gambler, blackleg, and coward." Among her effects was a Bible that had been presented to Earp when he was in Dodge. The inscription read: "To Wyatt S. Earp as a slight recognition of his many Christian virtues and steady following in the footsteps of the meek and lowly Jesus."

Amen.

We have come at last to our sixth Horrible, a slight, short, buck-toothed, narrow-shouldered youth whose slouch adds to his unwholesome appearance. He looks like a cretin, but this may be deceptive. As we crane cautiously forward, we can see that his label reads

 BILLY

The Kid
—a Rorschach ink blot

CHAPTER 6

This young outlaw is less interesting as a human being than as a sort of glorified Rorschach ink blot by which one may elicit fantasies and so judge their inventors. It is safe to say that at least a thousand writers have used Billy the Kid as a vessel into which to pour their passions, prejudices, and opinions; but it is likely that no two portraits of him jibe. He has been endowed with every imaginable personality; from the way he has been described one could conclude that he was the original Man with a Thousand Faces; his alleged background is as various. If his attrib-

117

uted names were to be listed as they would appear in a telephone book, they would look like this:

Antrim, Austin
Antrim, Henry
Antrim, William
Bonner, William
Bonney, William
LeRoy, William
McCarthy, Michael
McCarthy, William
McCarty, Henry
McCarty, Michael

The best guess is that he was born November 23, 1859, in New York City, and called Henry McCarty. There was an older brother, Joe. Around 1863 the family went west to Coffeyville, Kansas. The father may have died here; at all events, Mrs. Catherine McCarty was married on March 1, 1873, with her two sons as witnesses, to William H. Antrim, in Santa Fe, New Mexico. The newlyweds settled in Silver City, near the Arizona border, and here Mrs. Antrim died on September 16, 1874. Henry McCarty was not yet fifteen.

He killed for the first time three years later: a blacksmith called Windy Cahill, in a saloon near Camp Grant, Arizona. There followed some gambling, and some horse-stealing. Next he was a principal figure in the celebrated Lincoln County War, an affair which, including skirmishes and at least one pitched battle, went on for more than a year. The villains of this "war" were politicians, involved in their customary muttonheaded struggle for power, and guilty of their customary nonfeasance, misfeasance, and malfeasance. The Kid seems to have been caught up in it chiefly because he wasn't old enough to know any better. Several persons were killed in the course of this "war," and the Kid may have killed one or more of them; none can say for sure. In any case, his side lost, and for the rest of his brief life he was an outlaw, a hunted man.

He stole some more livestock. He probably killed a man named Joe Grant, after a brawl in a saloon. He rode with some exceedingly case-hardened characters, including Hendry Brown and Dave Rudabaugh. (Brown left him around 1880 to ride north into Kansas. He got a job on the police force of Caldwell, a cowtown, and before long he was marshal. He was so popular that the mayor presented him with a handsome, gold-mounted Winchester rifle for "valuable services rendered the citizens of Caldwell." In April, 1884, Marshal Brown, his deputy, and two other men tried to rob a bank at Medicine Lodge. Brown was shot down, the others were hanged, and the citizens of Caldwell subsequently discovered that their marshal had been corrupt the whole time he had worn their star. Rudabaugh was one of the would-be train robbers caught by Bat Masterson in 1878.)

Sheriff Pat Garrett and a posse first caught the Kid near Stinking Springs. He stood trial for murder, was found guilty, and was sentenced to be hanged. There were two men guarding him in the jail at Lincoln, but the Kid managed to get hold of a gun and killed them both.

Garrett, implacable, continued his pursuit. One brightly moonlit night he shot and killed the Kid in the bedroom of a ranch near Fort Sumner, New Mexico. It was July 14, 1881. Henry McCarty, alias William Bonney, alias the Kid, was not yet twenty-two.

And now the fun began.

The first book about him was dated July 15, 1881 and was subtitled *The history of an outlaw who killed a man for every year in his life,* a piece of fiction which was subsequently embroidered by nine out of ten of the writers who followed. The author of this book was a man named Fable, appropriately enough, and he described the Kid as wearing "a blue dragoon jacket of the finest broadcloth, heavily loaded down with gold embroidery, buckskin pants, dyed a jet black, with small tinkling bells sewed down the sides . . . drawers of fine scarlet broadcloth . . . and a hat covered with gold and jewels . . ."

The *Police Gazette* published a biography, too, as did Pat Garrett. Both liberally poured gore over the Kid. Garrett added a nice touch: he said that Billy, to show his skill, once shot the heads off several snowbirds, one after another. (J. Frank Dobie has remarked tartly, of this story, that it didn't happen because it couldn't happen.)

By 1889 a Frenchman, the Baron de Mandat-Grancey, had written a wondrous book called *La Brèche aux Buffles* —this was his way of saying Buffalo Gap—in which he reported how Billy the Kid killed his prison guard, a man named William Bonny. Other accounts appeared: the Kid had been a dishwasher in his youth; no, he had been a bootblack in New York City's Fourth Ward; no, he had

120

Garrett killed Billy—and the fun began

gone to college in the East and was really an Ivy League type.

The number of his killings mounted steadily. Soon he had killed twenty-three men, one for each of his own twenty-three years, not counting seven Mexicans whom he shot "just to see them kick." A play about him opened in 1906 and it ran for years. By 1918 its producers claimed it had been seen by ten million people. It was in 1906, too, that a dime novel appeared in which the Kid was described as an Apache who had been killed by Buffalo Bill, assisted by Wild Bill Hickok.

Then, oddly, the Kid dropped out of sight for a generation. When he reappeared, he had been twenty-four years old at the time of his death, and killed twenty-four men. Walter Noble Burns sentimentalized him so successfully that Hollywood brought out the first of some twenty movies about him. (Of these the two best-known, perhaps, are those that starred Robert Taylor and Jane Russell.) Somebody made up the wonderful story that the gun Garrett had used to kill the Kid was the same gun worn by Wild Bill Hickok when he was shot in Deadwood. Somebody else wrote that the judge who sentenced the Kid ordered him to be hanged by the neck until "you are dead, dead, dead," to which Billy retorted, "You go to hell, hell, hell!"

Pat Garrett, implacable lawman

The further away the mythmakers got from him, the more precisely they described him. He was "a boy of talent and exceptional intelligence," "good-natured and of a happy, carefree disposition," with "an unusually attractive personality." He was also "an adenoidal moron, both constitutionally and emotionally inadequate to a high degree." He killed forty-five men. He never killed anybody.

He was driven to a life of crime because, at the age of twelve, he killed a man who made a slurring remark to his mother. "His blue-gray eyes at times could turn cold and deadly." Pat Garrett never shot him at all, that night at Fort Sumner, for he was still alive in 1920, when he was known as Walk-Along Smith.

In one sense, it is of course perfectly true that Billy the Kid did not die. He is the most imperishable of our folk heroes. He will always be exploited by the commercialism of our popular entertainment media. Under his name there will always appear, whenever appropriate, a figure freshly refurbished so as to embody the hero who appropriately symbolizes the need of the hour: brutal killer, avenging angel, mama's boy, slayer of capitalist dragons, bewildered cat's paw, or gay, gallant, carefree cowpoke.

He can even be used, as in Michael McClure's avant-garde play, *The Beard,* to cavort obscenely with another American archetype, Jean Harlow, and so serve as a symbol of the decadence and impotence of latter-day America.

The face is blank, but it comes complete with a Handy Do-It-Yourself Kit so that the features may be easily filled in.

CHAPTER 7

THE WILDNESS OF WESTERNS

In the summer of 1911, Owen Wister took his family to Jackson Hole, Wyoming, for a holiday. His novel, *The Virginian*, had been published nine years before. One of his children, Fanny Kemble Wister, who edited his journals and letters (*Owen Wister Out West,* The University of Chicago Press, 1958), has recalled that "Everybody in the West seemed to have read *The Virginian*, and as soon as they heard my father's name would speak to him about it." She adds, of the novel, "It was written as fiction but has become history."

Hers is not a solitary judgment. Writing for *Harper's Magazine* in December, 1955, Bernard DeVoto cited *The*

125

Virginian as the first horse opera and claimed for Wister
the invention of the walkdown, at least as a fictional de-
vice. (The walkdown is the Wild, Wild West duello, span-
gled with suspense, in which hero and villain face each
other, usually across a sunbaked plaza whence all but they
have fled. In a ritual as conventional as a Japanese Nō
play, the villain draws, fires first, and misses narrowly,
after which the hero fires once and finally.)

But was Wister really the literary
inventor of the walkdown? The
same *Harper's Magazine*
printed in 1867 a thrilling
account by George Ward Nichols
of a walkdown in which James
(Wild Bill) B. Hickok gunned
one Dave Tutt. Nor will it avail
to protest that Nichols was
a reporter describing an
actual event; for over the
years it has been shown
that many of the
other incidents
reported by Nichols
in his article on Hickok
were wild fictions: who can
say that Nichols did not invent
the walkdown as well? Wister
wrote fiction; it has become
history, Nichols wrote reportage;
it has been demonstrated to be
fiction. No clear line can be
drawn. Where there should be a
sharp distinction, there is only
fuzz.

This immensely inconsequential
issue serves to point up a very
real difficulty posed by the
literature of the Wild,
Wild West. How can the
common reader split out what is

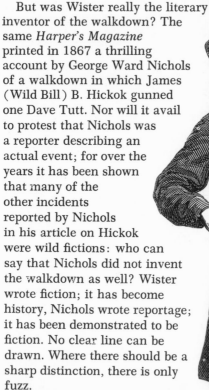

126

Wild Bill, as portrayed in *Harper's Magazine*

history and biography in this literature from what is fiction? It is a task that severely taxes the library cataloguist, who must decide where such-and-such a book should be shelved; how much more it must daunt the common reader! Which tale springs from the author's imagination? Which from legend? Which from imperfect memory? Which from such documented sources as may exist—court records, say, or contemporary newspaper accounts, or letters? A thick mist hugs the Great Plains, and no guide lives who can lead us surefootedly over the trails that were so clear less than a century ago.

Perhaps the best way to grasp the complexity of the problem is to turn the pages of a bibliography of publications about Western bad men compiled by Ramon F. Adams (*Six-Guns & Saddle Leather,* The University of Oklahoma Press, 1954). Here is a book to abash those who are hopeful about human nature and delight those who are cynical. No more striking evidence could be offered of the lengths to which *Homo sapiens* will go to avoid harsh fact so that he may wallow in titillative fancy. Mr. Adams for many years collected books about Western bad men; as a bibliographer he was obliged to study the contents of those books. "Never would I have believed," he writes, "that so much false, inaccurate, and garbled history could have found its way into print." The melancholy fact is that the books which sell best are precisely the books which are least trustworthy. Of the 1,132 books and pamphlets listed by Mr. Adams in his bibliography, he can confidently apply the adjective "reliable" to only about two dozen, and these few are, in the main, pamphlets privately printed or books published by university presses. Come to think of it, this may not be such a poor average, at that.

After poking about industriously in the compost of Western literature, Mr. Adams grouped its authors under four headings: (1) the nickel and dime novelists—employed by *The National Police Gazette,* the Beadle Library, and their several rivals and imitators—whose use of words like "true" and "authentic" in the titles of their œuvres is, as Mr. Adams suggests, a sure guarantee of brummagem; (2) the old-timers who wrote their so-called reminiscences; (3) the "rocking-chair historians," who have neither the

energy to dig out their facts at first hand nor the skepticism to evaluate their facts at second hand; and (4) the
tiny handful of able, conscientious historians who have
somehow stumbled upon this grade-school Grand Guignol.

But, as Mr. Adams himself surely recognizes, his com-
partments are not watertight. Take, for example, Burton
Rascoe's biography of Belle Starr (*Belle Starr, "the Bandit
Queen,"* Random House, 1941), of which Mr. Adams notes
that it is "the most complete and reliable work done on this
female bandit to date." This superlative must be appre-
hended not as praise for Rascoe's book but as denigration
of all other works dealing with the Bandit Queen. There is
no question but that Rascoe diligently ran to earth all the
available facts about his subject. Indeed, in an exceedingly
entertaining essay on folklore and history, which prefaces
the biography, he demonstrated persuasively how the personal memory of old-timers, complete with vivid detail,
can turn out embarrassingly often to be merely a rehash of
the fragrant sludge purveyed by *The National Police Gazette*. (Rascoe was fortunate enough to have, ready at
hand, a complete file of the publication against which he
could check his old-timers' tales. Other chroniclers of the
Wild, Wild West, not so well equipped, have in consequence often been outrageously flimflammed.)

But then, spang in the middle of this preface, Rascoe
gravely informs us that Frank James, Jesse's older brother,
was convicted and sentenced to serve a term in the penitentiary for his crimes. He goes further. He supplies us
with details: how many years James spent in jail (eighteen), and even how he was occupied (in making burlap
bags) while he was confined. James was, however, neither
convicted nor sentenced. Such an egregious blunder tends
to make the reader wary of Rascoe's other statements, and
leads him to regard "reliable" as a relative term.

Two of the better books about Jesse James were written
by Robertus Love (*The Rise and Fall of Jesse James*, G. P.
Putnam's Sons, 1926) and Homer Croy (*Jesse James Was
My Neighbor*, Duell, Sloan and Pearce, 1949). Both men
sentimentalize their subject, but neither can be charged
with being a rocking-chair historian. Mr. Croy was particularly zealous in retracing Jesse's steps and in looking up
elderly folk who could supply vivid details. Yet both men

Frank James
—he never made bags from burlap

129

soberly ladle out the preposterous yarn about Jesse's saving
the widow whose mortgage was about to be foreclosed, a
tale for which there is not a jot of evidence. Perhaps another category must be set up, to comprise all the writers
who are too tenderhearted to kill a good story.

One of the best ways to appreciate how the literature of
the West can plunge the common reader into a puzzlement
is to survey what has been written, one way or another,
about Wyatt Earp, whose commanding figure dominates
the landscape from the cowtowns of Kansas to Tombstone,
Arizona, and north to the mining camps of Colorado. Earp,
unlike most gunslingers, lived a long life, dying only some
forty years ago. A year later his first biography appeared
(*Wyatt Earp, Frontier Marshal*, Houghton, Mifflin, 1931),
written by Stuart Lake. It is an extremely skillful book.
One well-developed scene follows upon another, each an
occasion of unexampled bravery, and in each the reader's
emotions are enlisted on behalf of the quiet-spoken, clear-
eyed, grim-lipped Marshal Earp, champion of law and
order. Many long passages in the book are direct quota-
tions from Earp himself, revealing him to speak in a prose
remindful of Mr. Lake's own supple literary style. Nor
should this astonish, for Mr. Lake revealed, in a letter to
Burton Rascoe, that he had undertaken to spruce up Earp's
speech somewhat, in the interests of greater readability.
(Earp appears, in truth, to have been rather poorly edu-
cated.)

If Mr. Lake's biography fails to convince, it is because
his subject is presented as so infallible, so surpassingly
heroic. At one point Mr. Lake, as it were, admits us as
witnesses while he interviews his man:

" 'Did you ever lose a fight?' I asked him.

" 'Never,' he admitted, and in his simple answer there
was a measure of the man."

Mr. Lake's biography held the field alone for some little
time, seeping steadily into the stuff of history.

But of course the process of establishing a hero neces-
sarily entails demolishing a villain and, as Earp told the
tale to Mr. Lake, the villain was the Texas cowboy,
drunken, pugnacious, and treacherous. If Earp were to
build up a record for his biographer as a verray parfit gentil
knyght, it could only be by telling him how he had maced

those terrible Texans on the noggin with the barrel of his
Colt Peacemaker. At this juncture, as though to make the
historical record more entertaining by injecting the necessary element of conflict, there appeared the chroniclers of
the cow kingdoms who, upon hearing Earp's statements as
reported by Mr. Lake, said in effect, " 'Twarn't so."

One of the first defenders of the cowboys was Eugene
Cunningham. His profiles of Western killers (*Triggernometry, a Gallery of Gunfighters*, The Press of the Pioneers,
1934), written in a nice, smooth, take-it-easy prose, down-
graded Earp considerably from the pedestal on which he
had been perched by Mr. Lake. Next there came along the
late Dr. Floyd B. Streeter, librarian of Kansas State College
at Fort Hays, with a volume (*Prairie Trails & Cow Towns*,
Chapman & Grimes, 1936) in which he flatly denied, after
painstaking investigation, that Earp had, as alleged, anything to do with calming the fevers of Ellsworth, one of the
early Kansas cowtowns.

The issue was now joined. Wild, Wild West buffs were
now either Earp believers or Earp apostates. Gathered into
societies in New York, Chicago, Denver, Los Angeles, and
elsewhere, they met and discussed Earp with heat. (Their
societies are often called posses; their chairmen are sometimes called sheriffs. Each posse regularly issues bulletins in
which are printed speculations about various notables of
the Wild, Wild West.) By 1946 Frank Waters had published, as one of the Rivers of America series, *The Colorado* (Rinehart & Co., 1946), in which for the first time it
was suggested that Wyatt Earp had brought a wife to
Tombstone and deserted her there. The temperature rose
in the rooms where the posses of Westerners met.

It rose still further when a book by Joe Chisholm (*Brewery Gulch*, The Naylor Company, 1949) was posthumously
published, for here there was printed the flat accusation
that a clique organized and directed by Wyatt Earp had
systematically looted the stages bound from Tombstone.
But the next year there appeared a book (*The Last Chance*,
E. P. Dutton, 1950) by John Myers Myers that restored the
balance. Mr. Myers had written a first-rate social history of
Tombstone in which he sedulously embroidered the gospel
of Wyatt Earp according to Mr. Lake. In 1952, moreover,
Stanley Vestal published his entertaining history of Dodge

City (*Queen of Cowtowns*, Harper & Brothers) in which he both borrowed generously from Mr. Lake and also returned what he had borrowed with interest. Still more recently, Richard O'Connor has written a biography of Bat Masterson (*Bat Masterson*, Doubleday, 1957) in which there is likewise much use made of material from Mr. Lake's book. (It should also be said that Mr. O'Connor was happy to include, in his portrait of Masterson, as many of the warts and blemishes as he was able to find; in terms of Western biography, this is indeed a new and auspicious development.)

And then Frank Waters published his angry attack on the whole edifice of the Earp legend (*The Earp Brothers of Tombstone*, Clarkson Potter, 1960) in which he turned that legend inside out. He painted Earp not as marshal and hero, but as a bigamist, confidence man, killer, and conniving villain of deepest dye.

Which is the truer picture? It must be conceded that Mr. Lake's picture is the one that has been traced over the face of the West. And if Mr. Waters' picture is the more accurate, why, then, as he says, what greater irony than that Wyatt Earp, confidence man, in death should have contrived his slickest trick, to have bamboozled the whole republic into accepting him as a story-book marshal!

It may be that what can be detected here—in the books by Mr. Adams, Mr. Waters, Mr. O'Connor, and a few others—is the first foreshadowing of a trend. Perhaps at long last the Wild, Wild West is in for some very belated and very badly needed critical scrutiny. There are, praise be, other recent books about Westerners which are casting a welcome shadow.

Take the case of Billy the Kid. A few years ago Jefferson C. Dykes compiled a list (*Billy the Kid, the bibliography of a legend*, The University of New Mexico Press, 1952) of the books, magazine articles, motion pictures, plays, ballads, phonograph records, and comic books dealing with the Kid. There were four hundred and thirty-seven entries in Mr. Dykes's collection, the harvest of the first half-century after the Kid's death, and quite probably none of them was worth much from the standpoint of historical veracity. But in the last few years a few reasonably careful books

This Week! A New Story by PERCY B. ST. JOHN.   A New Story by HAL STANDISH This Week.

THE GOLDEN WEEKLY

Vol. II.   NEW YORK. JULY 9. 1891.   No. 87

A periodical embellishment

have appeared. Frazier Hunt, under the tutelage of the late Maurice G. Fulton, gathered at first hand the material for a biography (*The Tragic Days of Billy the Kid,* Hastings House, 1956) which, while fleshed out with some rather mawkish assumptions, nevertheless has the bones of truth.

Even better, William A. Keleher has written a history (*Violence in Lincoln County, 1869–1881*, The University of New Mexico Press, 1957) which is a model of how to assemble and present the materials of a Western story. Mr. Keleher, who has given this work of impressive scholarship the disarming subtitle, *A New Mexico Item*, has moreover had the good sense to reduce the Kid to scale, so that he becomes simply one figure in a complex, violent, and gripping narrative. Anyone who has a mind to undertake the further chronicling of some bloody chapter out of the history of the Wild, Wild West could not better begin than by studying how Mr. Keleher has done this job.

There is of course much other good work in the field: writing which is, for the author's part, conscientious and, for the reader's part, highly entertaining. Even so short a survey as this one should not ignore Wayne Gard's biography of Sam Bass, Texas' favorite outlaw (*Sam Bass*, Houghton, Mifflin, 1936), nor Struthers Burt's contribution to the Rivers of America series (*Powder River, Let 'er Buck*, Farrar & Rinehart, 1938), which includes as good an account of the Johnson County War as can be found anywhere. (It was the Johnson County War which, after a fashion, inspired Owen Wister's *The Virginian*.) Further, James D. Horan has with some delight impaled the more outrageous legends about most of the alleged heroes and heroines of the Wild, Wild West in two extremely entertaining books, *Desperate Men* (G. P. Putnam's 1948) and *Desperate Women* (G. P. Putnam's, 1952).

Least of all should one ignore Joseph Henry Jackson's account of California bandits (*Bad Company*, Harcourt, Brace, 1949), for Mr. Jackson brings to his task all the qualities one could hope for in a writer about Western bad men: careful scholarship, a lucid prose style, a healthy skepticism about even his primary sources, and—rarest of all—wit. Those who pick up *Bad Company* are in for a most pleasant evening. They will meet again, among others, Black Bart, who should be everybody's favorite road agent.

Unfortunately the Black Barts come few and far between in this world, whether it be of the Wild, Wild West or not. In the main, the characters who figure prominently

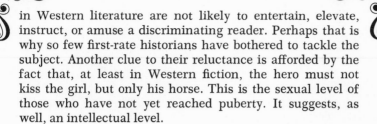

in Western literature are not likely to entertain, elevate, instruct, or amuse a discriminating reader. Perhaps that is why so few first-rate historians have bothered to tackle the subject. Another clue to their reluctance is afforded by the fact that, at least in Western fiction, the hero must not kiss the girl, but only his horse. This is the sexual level of those who have not yet reached puberty. It suggests, as well, an intellectual level.

Cowboys and their horses at full gallop

The code forbade shooting from behind

CHAPTER 8

THE WILD, WILD WEST

A SUMMARY

What, in summary, of the world of the Wild, Wild West? Manifestly, it was an underworld, corrupt and rotten. Its heroes, vaunted for their courage, in fact showed only the rashness of the alcoholic or the desperation of the cornered rat. They were popularly supposed to have honored the Wild West's so-called code, which forbade the shooting of an unarmed man and likewise the shooting of an armed man until he had been faced and warned of the peril in which he stood. But look at our half-dozen, the most celebrated heroes of all:

Murieta, if indeed he ever existed, is known only by legend and so may be ignored.

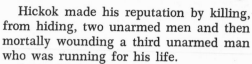

Hickok made his reputation by killing, from hiding, two unarmed men and then mortally wounding a third unarmed man who was running for his life.

Jesse James at least twice murdered unarmed bank tellers, not because they had offered resistance but when they were cowering at the bandit's feet.

Wyatt Earp and his brothers, shielded by police badges, provoked a fight, shot first, and killed men who, according to three eyewitnesses, were holding up their hands.

Bat Masterson is saved from any similar charge chiefly because he was such a poor shot.

Billy the Kid shot and killed from ambush, not once, but several times. In-

An evening of ease in the West

141

Fights were provoked on occasion

Heroes of the Republic

deed, only the first of his authenticated killings seems to have come about in man-to-man fight, and even on that occasion his opponent was unarmed.

What heroes, to be exalted by the Republic!

As outlaws they were first adored because, it was argued, they robbed only the railroad monopolist and the banker, the men most heartily hated west of the Missis-

sippi. As law officers they were first adored because, it was argued, they enforced the peace in perilous circumstances, against overwhelming odds. Both propositions are cock-eyed. Outlaw or law officer, it made little difference, they were one brutal brotherhood. The so-called law officers more often caused than quelled crime. Hendry Brown, an outlaw in New Mexico, could ride to Kansas and pin on a sheriff's star; Jim Younger, an outlaw in Missouri, could ride to Texas and pin on a deputy sheriff's star; even Billy the Kid rode for a time as a member of a sheriff's posse and, had his side won the Lincoln County War, might well have come down to us in folklore as a force for law and order. The whole boodle of them careened through lives of unredeemed violence and vulgarity, to fetch up—where else?—in the Valhalla of the comics, the movies, and television.

Television in particular would seem to have inherited the august mantle of *The National Police Gazette*. The parallels between the two mass media are striking. The *Gazette* preached each week a superficial, meretricious ethic; so do the televised entertainments that deal with the West. The *Gazette*'s editor was not concerned with the facts of the matters his journal reported but only with the number of his readers; the producers of the televised entertainments fill his shoes precisely. He was successful; so, as Nielsen is their judge, are they. He worked out a formula for populating the American pantheon; so have they. It is the master's recipe, only slightly sauced to make the stew more palatable for those who have had instilled in them the democratic ethos. Thus, on television the hero must protect such underdogs as the Mexican, the Indian, and the Chinese from the acquisitive Anglo-Saxon upperdog, a behavior which, in terms of historical fact, is ludicrously fanciful.

And even granting the assumption that the purveyors of this sludge are concerned not with history but with legend, what a shameful and ghastly legend it is! to be despised, if not on the sufficient grounds of its ugly violence, then on the grounds of its even uglier vulgarity.

The moral, of course, is that crime, when commercially exploited, *does* pay, and the more sadistic the better. The Wild, Wild West, as exploited by irresponsible men—from Richard K. Fox of *The National Police Gazette* to the television producers of today—who care not a hang for the truth of history so long as they can count their audiences in the scores of millions, have created for the world an enduring image of America.

Over it there hangs the stink of evil.

SELECTED BIBLIOGRAPHY

ADAMS, RAMON F., *Six-Guns & Saddle Leather*, The University of Oklahoma Press, 1954.

BURNS, WALTER NOBLE, *The Robin Hood of El Dorado*, Coward-McCann, 1932.

————, *The Saga of Billy the Kid*, Doubleday & Page, 1926.

BURT, STRUTHERS, *Powder River, Let 'er Buck*, Farrar & Rinehart, 1938.

CHISHOLM, JOE, *Brewery Gulch*, The Naylor Company, 1949.

CLEMENS, SAMUEL L., *Roughing It*, Harper & Brothers, 1899.

CONNELLEY, WILLIAM E., *Wild Bill and His Era*, The Press of the Pioneers, 1933.

CROY, HOMER, *Jesse James Was My Neighbor*, Duell, Sloan and Pearce, 1949.

CUNNINGHAM, EUGENE, *Triggernometry: A Gallery of Gun-fighters*, The Press of the Pioneers, 1934.

DEVOTO, BERNARD, "The Easy Chair," *Harper's*, December, 1955.

DOBIE, J. FRANK, *A Vaquero of the Brush Country*, The Southwest Press, 1929.

———, Editor, *Southwestern Lore*, Publications of the Texas Folk-Lore Society, Number IX, The Southwest Press, 1931.

DRAGO, HARRY SINCLAIR, *Wild, Woolly & Wicked*, Clarkson N. Potter, 1960.

DYKES, JEFFERSON C., *Billy The Kid: The Bibliography of a Legend*, The University of New Mexico Press, 1952.

GARD, WAYNE, *Sam Bass*, Houghton Mifflin, 1936.

———, *The Chisholm Trail*, The University of Oklahoma Press, 1954.

HOLBROOK, STEWART, *The Story of American Railroads*, Crown, 1947.

HORAN, JAMES D., *Desperate Men*, G. P. Putnam's Sons, 1949.

———, *Desperate Women*, G. P. Putnam's Sons, 1952.

HUNT, FRAZIER, *The Tragic Days of Billy the Kid*, Hastings House, 1956.

JACKSON, JOSEPH H., *Bad Company*, Harcourt, Brace, 1949.

JAMESON, HENRY B., *Miracle of the Chisholm Trail*, Tri-State Centennial Commission, 1967(?).

JENNEWEIN, J. LEONARD, *Calamity Jane of the Western Trails*, Dakota Books, 1953.

KELEHER, WILLIAM A., *Violence in Lincoln County: A New Mexico Item*, The University of New Mexico Press, 1957.

LAKE, STUART, *Wyatt Earp, Frontier Marshal*, Houghton Mifflin, 1931.

LOVE, ROBERTUS, *The Rise and Fall of Jesse James*, G. P. Putnam's Sons, 1926.

McCOY, JOSEPH G., *Historic Sketches of the Cattle Trade of the West and Southwest*, edited by Ralph P. Bieber, Arthur H. Clark Company, 1940.

MYERS, JOHN MYERS, *The Last Chance*, E. P. Dutton, 1950.

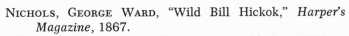

NICHOLS, GEORGE WARD, "Wild Bill Hickok," *Harper's Magazine*, 1867.

O'CONNOR, RICHARD, *Bat Masterson*, Doubleday, 1957.

RASCOE, BURTON, *Belle Starr, "The Bandit Queen,"* Random House, 1941.

STREETER, FLOYD B., *Prairie Trails & Cow Towns*, Chapman & Grimes, 1936.

VERCKLER, STEWART P., *Cowtown Abilene 1867–1875*, privately printed, 1966(?).

VESTAL, STANLEY, *Queen of Cowtowns*, Harper & Brothers, 1952.

WATERS, FRANK, *The Colorado*, Rinehart & Company, 1946.

————, *The Earp Brothers of Tombstone*, Clarkson N. Potter, 1960.

WERSTEIN, IRVING, *Marshal Without a Gun*, Julian Messner, 1959.

WILSTACH, FRANK J., *Wild Bill Hickok, Prince of Pistoleers*, Doubleday & Page, 1926.

WISTER, FANNY KEMBLE, *Owen Wister Out West*, The University of Chicago Press, 1958.

INDEX